WRITING ROMANTIC FICTION

The Essential Guide

Need
— 2 —
Know

Writing Romantic Fiction – The Essential Guide is also available in accessible formats for people with any degree of sight loss. The large print edition and ebook (with accessibility features enabled) are available from Need2Know. Please let us know if there are any special features you require and we will do our best to accommodate your needs.

This new revised edition is published in Great Britian in 2011 by
Need2Know
Remus House
Coltsfoot Drive
Peterborough
PE2 9BF
Telephone 01733 898103
Fax 01733 313524
www.need2knowbooks.co.uk

Contents

Introduction 5

Chapter 1   Loving Your Genre............................ 9

Chapter 2   Beginners' Questions 15

Chapter 3   Chapter One 25

Chapter 4   Believable Characters....................33

Chapter 5   The Language of Love..................... 41

Chapter 6   Appealing to the Senses 49

Chapter 7   Putting in the Steam 57

Chapter 8   Values - Old and New......................67

Chapter 9   Research..75

Chapter 10   Getting It All Together....................83

Chapter 11   Surviving Rejection......................... 91

Chapter 12   Before and After Publication 99

Chapter 13   Tips from the Top...........................107

Chapter 14   Let's be Practical........................... 117

Chapter 15   The American Romance Market................127

Chapter 16   Further Help...................................139

Help List 147

Book List 151

Introduction

Do I hear the cynics among you say that romance is dead? Not for the millions of readers who find escape between the covers of a paperback novel, whether it's the standard 192 pages of a Mills & Boon or Silhouette romance, or the longer, lushly illustrated historical sagas on the shelves of any bookstore or newsagent.

Look again at those bookshelves. Or at the crowded sections of the romance novels at any public library. Romantic fiction has never been healthier nor more popular.

Now take a moment to analyse why it should be so. Isn't it a fact that love, the prime ingredient of every romantic novel, is the universal element with which we can all identify? Who has ever known at first hand the imagined drama of a science fiction setting? How many of us have personally experienced the espionage, the murders, the western adventures so beloved of those particular genres? Comparatively few, compared with the great mass of the reading public.

But we've all felt the joys and pangs of love at some stage in our lives, whether it's romantic love, love for a child, for parents or animals. So immediately we're familiar and comfortable with the love story ahead of us. The young girl reading her first romance can understand the emotions portrayed in the same way as an older woman.

One will be looking forward and one looking back, but they will both share in the heroine's experiences, because the feelings expressed are common to all women. We open the covers of our chosen novel with a feeling of anticipation, knowing that boy will meet girl, lose girl, find girl again, and both will reach their happy ending . . .

But that essence of familiarity is just where the author's craft takes over. If it were as simple as I've just described, every book would be a carbon copy of the one before it. What makes each one a story to be remembered long after the covers are closed is each author's individual voice.

'Do I hear the cynics among you say that romance is dead? Not for the millions of readers who find escape between the covers of a paperback novel.'

Just for fun I asked a group of women to give me a snap definition of a romantic novel. Most of the replies were flippant. Some were unprintable. Here are a few of them:

- 'A lot of mush with a sloppy ending.'

- 'A jolly good read, with a proper beginning, middle and end, like a book should be.'

- 'All sex in them, and no real story.'

- 'Better nowadays than the old soppy ones, and more realistic.'

- 'Never read them - prefer whodunnits.'

- 'They're all right if the characters are believable and don't do things no ordinary person would ever do.'

- 'Nice to curl up with in bed.'

I could have added a few more definitions of my own, but the one I keep uppermost in my mind when I'm writing a romantic novel is that it's essentially the story of two people falling in love, but for whom the path of true love *never* runs smoothly.

Romantic novels have come a long way since such classic tales as *Jane Eyre* and *Wuthering Heights,* and in recent years, as the popularity of the genre soars, styles in fiction have been as unpredictable as styles in the fashion world.

'Gothics' can make way for lusty 'bodice-rippers' and then suddenly all the demand is for chaste and gentle stories. Backgrounds as diverse as the Greek Islands or the Scottish Highlands or the American Civil War can be out of favour for a while and then be all the rage.

But what never changes are the emotions and feelings between a man and a woman who are falling in love. This is the major point to remember for every aspiring romantic novelist. And that's really what romantic fiction is all about.

The comment about every book needing a good beginning, middle and end is a point to be remembered. Combine that with attractive characters and the essential conflict between them, and you've got the basis for every romantic novel.

'Romantic novels have come a long way since such classic tales as *Jane Eyre* and *Wuthering Heights.'*

6

How you get your characters to their happy ending - by constantly throwing the lovers together and simultaneously putting obstacles in their path, but in such a way that these events seem perfectly logical and yet look neither contrived nor ridiculous - is part of the novelist's craft.

The reader must always be in some doubt that all will turn out well, even if, deep down, she knows that it will! That's the stuff of which romantic novels are made, but to make your reader doubt the final outcome until the last few pages and then convince her that the events couldn't have happened in any other way is probably the hardest part of writing this kind of novel.

In the following pages, I hope to make things a little clearer for everyone who has ever dreamed of putting pen to paper and doesn't know where to begin. And remember that the most glittering names in the romantic fiction world had to begin somewhere.

None of us was born a writer, however glamorous that may sound. It's a craft to be learned, and one that can bring immense pleasure and satisfaction.

'None of us was born a writer, however glamorous that may sound. It's a craft to be learned, and one that can bring immense pleasure and satisfaction.'

Chapter One
Loving Your Genre

So you want to write romantic novels. If you think it's a quick way to make your fortune, forget it. If you think it's easy to dash off something that looks so simple a child could do it, don't forget it, but think again.

The author of such a novel is experienced in creating that very impression of simplicity, and the reader is, and should be, totally unaware of the skill that has gone into it. It's a sad fact that critics scoff at our 'love stories'. It's an even truer fact that most of them admit that they can't write them. You want more statistics? Hundreds of romantic novels arrive at publishers' offices every week. Most of them are rejected. But don't let that deter you. If you want to write romantic novels badly enough, then you'll persevere and the pleasure it will bring you will make it all worthwhile.

I've read many unpublished manuscripts from beginners, and one of the most frequent faults is trying to be too literary. Beginners will often search for an obscure word in an attempt to be clever where a short, vivid word would convey a far clearer meaning. Romantic readers aren't morons, but their prime reason for choosing these novels is entertainment.

It's perfectly true that, in creating a believable background and perhaps working in some old country folklore or new and fascinating profession, the writer expands the reader's knowledge painlessly. The art is in not making it seem like a lesson, but in adding another dimension to what is still basically a love story.

And getting rich quick? Yes, for the lucky few there *are* fortunes to be made in writing romantic fiction. But for every one who makes it to the top, there are thousands who never even get published. There are many more who tick over nicely, reaping the rewards of their self-discipline. And for all of us there is the enticement that one day *our* book will be a bestseller.

But that's the catch. What one author pens as an original phrase can quickly become clichéd if copied almost word for word. Readers quickly become disenchanted and complain that the books are 'all the same'. And who wants to have people saying that your book is just like someone else's? Certainly not the editors.

Original writing is more precious than gold to editors who have read it before. New authors who think for themselves without aping the one who happens to be in vogue will always get a more hopeful reading at busy publishing houses.

Don't ever write your first romance - or any subsequent one - with your tongue in your cheek, feeling that this is a genre slightly beneath you but you'll give it a try, anyway. Believe me, it will show!

'Don't ever write your first romance – or any subsequent one – with your tongue in your cheek, feeling that this is a genre slightly beneath you.'

Editors are highly intelligent and professional people who will spot insincerity immediately. They are also inundated with unsolicited manuscripts from hopeful authors. You're undoubtedly entering the most competitive of all the writing genres, but if you have the staying power and the drive, and that special talent that gives you the insight into characters and their motivation, then you're off to a good start.

Know your market

To know and understand your market is half the battle. To be able to identify with your heroine is essential, but you must also know your other characters through and through. If you went to a party and knew only one person, wouldn't you feel a little on the sidelines? It's the same in fiction. Get to know all your characters. Chapter 4 deals with developing and 'fleshing-out' the characters in more detail.

Romantic fiction is sometimes described as formula fiction. The only real formula involved is that two people are going to fall in love, confront various obstacles that will keep them apart, and eventually get together again. Simple, isn't it? If the formulae are to be decried, what about the good old western? Or the espionage novel? Or the whodunnit? There's nothing wrong in following in the footsteps that have gone before, as long as you give them your own mark.

Some publishers issue guidelines for potential authors which can be very helpful to beginners. But following these guidelines too closely can result in the manuscript being returned with the comment that this storyline has been done before. Do send for guidelines if they're available, but use them for what they are - a guide to the general requirements of that particular publishing house. Don't slavishly put in all the suggested characters - the stock housekeeper, the glossy other woman, the wimpish other man . . .

I can't speak for other authors, but I always finish writing my novels with a feeling of regret as well as satisfaction in bringing my hero and heroine to their happy ending. The characters and their environment that I've come to know are now on their own, and have to continue their lives without me. I know I will miss them.

Perhaps it all sounds a bit far-fetched. But it's my own fantasy world that I've created, and in doing so have tried to make my readers believe in it implicitly. To do that, I *must* believe in it myself. Readers must be totally convinced of the plausibility of the plot, of the qualities of the characters, of the progress of the book.

Romances have happy endings, whatever traumas the author has put the characters through to reach that point. They are an escape from reality, portraying life as it could be. For many readers, the novel is a wish-fulfilment.

There are many categories within the overall class of romantic fiction, and every beginner will find that one appeals more than another. My strongest advice would be to write the kind of books you enjoy reading, in either contemporary or historical fiction.

Whether you prefer to write a gentle romance or a steamier one, market study is essential. Apart from the very obvious differences of content and style, it should also be obvious that published novels vary in length.

Each publisher has particular requirements, from the short 55,000-word novel, to lengthy sagas of 250,000 words, and anything in-between. There is also a market for the novella of around 40,000 words. As a general rule, the longer the novel, the more intricate the plot needs to be.

Publishers' names and addresses can be found in any edition of the *Writers' and Artists' Yearbook* or *The Guide to Book Publishers* and every published novel gives details of its individual publisher.

'Romances have happy endings, whatever traumas the author has put the characters through to reach that point.'

Contemporary or historical?

Settings for contemporary novels can be anything that's applicable to today's lifestyle. Historical novels cover any period of time up to and including the Second World War.

There are many people who remember the Second World War - and the First - with great clarity, and are admirably fitted to write from personal recollection, thus saving the necessity of a good deal of research as to when ration books were abolished, or the New Look came into being, for instance! But don't assume you won't have to do any research - see chapter 9 for some of the possible pitfalls.

I wouldn't advise anyone to embark on a historical novel without possessing a love of history. It's too complex a genre to enter without an intense interest in the way people used to live, work, play, and even die; the tools they used, the clothes they wore; such diversions as country fairs; the language spoken in other times; the limitations in medical facilities; the vast class-consciousness; the outdated occupations from lamplighter to kiddley-boy . . . (What is a kiddley-boy? You could read *Killigrew Clay* by Rowena Summers to find out!)

The truly dedicated historical author will be totally fascinated by the seemingly small, insignificant incidents that have changed the course of history; and have an empathy for those long-dead men and women who probably never knew the far-reaching effects of their discoveries, their journeys, their researches.

The historical author puts a credible interpretation on such events, whether with real characters or fictional ones, and preferably with a skilful interweaving of the two. As in the contemporary novel, the characters should be so real in the author's mind that to the reader the book is all about real people. It all begins with the author.

Heavy going, isn't it? But a love of history for fictional purposes is more than memorising dates in chronological order, knowing who the Luddites were or where Florence Nightingale was born - if that happens to be relevant to your book. It's all that and more.

It's the ability to think yourself back into a bygone age, where life was not necessarily lived at a slower pace as some people so lovingly imagine.

Understand and sympathise, even with the least attractive of your characters. We are all, to some extent, a product of our environment, and Victorians, Elizabethans *et al* no less representative of theirs.

To portray them accurately, appreciate the differences in lifestyles, means of communication and travel, lighting, fashions, toys, food and drink, the etiquette . . . Daunted yet?

There are innumerable differences between people of 'then' and 'now', but there is also one illuminating similarity, and that is the ability to love, which is the essence of every romantic novel, the emotion that we all know and recognise.

Whatever else changes through the ages, the emotions that people feel are constant and universal, transcending race, religion and time.

Romantic novels reflect those feelings over and over, providing the reader with the means to escape from the everyday world. She's bright enough to know that it's fiction, but that escape may be all she has. Isn't it wonderful to know that you're writing a story that may enable some lonely woman to enjoy as vicarious fantasy the romance that may have long faded from her life?

So perhaps we're doing no more than putting TV soap operas on to paper. But we shouldn't downgrade our books. Some of the books that we regard as classics now - Thomas Hardy's novels, for example, would have been seen as the popular, even pulp fiction of their day.

One of the most gratifying things about being a writer is that you can begin at any age, with no class distinctions, the only real qualification being the ability to write something that other people want to read. You don't need to 'know somebody' in publishing or have a degree in English literature, though obviously attention to spelling and grammar is very important, if only to save the editorial headache in deciphering your script on a wet Monday morning. And, also, in order to compete with all those other authors who know that seeing a well-presented manuscript at least makes a busy editor feel a bit more hopeful at reading yet another unsolicited novel.

So if you still want to write a romance, let's begin at the beginning.

'Whatever else changes through the ages, the emotions that people feel are constant and universal, transcending race, religion and time.'

Summing Up

- Enjoy what you write. If you don't, it will show.
- Send for publishers' guidelines if available.
- Read what's being published now.
- Be critical about your own work, but not to the extent that you edit out every little thing you first liked.
- There's no formula, other than that two people are going to fall in love, meet many obstacles, and eventually reach their happy or hopeful ending.

Chapter Two
Beginners' Questions

Q. I've always wanted to write a romantic novel, but I haven't a clue how to go about it.

A. Novels can't exist without people. The characters are the life-blood of any novel, so begin by deciding who your central character is going to be. It will invariably be a female in a romantic novel. Write a character sketch of everything you can possibly think up about her: name, age, height, colouring, habits, occupation, family background, likes, dislikes, preferences in books and music, clothes, favourite film stars, pop stars, religion, education, political slant, etc.

You may only use a fraction of this information in your novel, but by the time you've filled a few pages with details about your character, you'll begin to know her. She'll start to become real to you. If your imagination isn't used to conjuring characters out of thin air, then find a suitable picture in a magazine and describe the girl in it. The picture will only give you the physical appearance, but it should spark you off by suggesting the questions you'll then ask yourself.

Who? Where? Why? What? How? By applying all of these to the suggestions above, you will finish with a detailed description of a lifestyle that is uniquely your creation.

Q. But how do I actually begin? I've never written anything more than letters to friends. Is it all right to write in longhand?

A. Perfectly all right as a first draft, but not for submission to a literary agent or publisher. Remember that this is a competitive market, and the busiest one of all. Agents and editors simply haven't the time to read hand-written scripts. Apart from which if all the others arriving on the desk are neatly typed, it's human nature to go for the most professional-looking ones first, isn't it?

'Novels can't exist without people. The characters are the life-blood of any novel, so begin by deciding who your central character is going to be.'

Briefly, your manuscript should be typed double-spaced, using one side of A4 paper, leaving about an inch margin at either side of the script, and also at top and bottom. Each page should be numbered consecutively. The title of the novel should be on the covering page, with your name and address and pseudonym, if any. Always take one copy, and with computers, always keep a backup copy. *The Writers' and Artists' Yearbook* covers this in more detail.

Q. You mentioned pseudonyms. Why do authors use them, and do you have one? Do I need one?

A. My pseudonyms are Jean Saunders, Jean Innes, Rowena Summers, Sally Blake and Jodi Nicol. It is entirely a personal choice whether or not you want to have your own name on the spine of a novel or a name that you've invented.

If you become prolific, you may write different types of book for various publishers. Sometimes a publisher jealously guards the name on the contract, and insists that you use another name if you write for anyone else. You may choose to do so, anyway.

I used to write teenage novels as Jean Saunders for William Heinemann. For racier novels, and eventually family sagas, for Severn House, I chose the name Rowena Summers in order not to confuse readers - and Jodi Nicol is strictly for erotica! I also write wartime sagas set in Cornwall as Rachel Moore.

Q. Isn't there a lot of sex in today's romantic novels? I don't want to write anything to embarrass my family!

A. Then don't. There's plenty of room for the more gentle romance. But I would say that in that case you do need to have a strong plot and to work it out carefully before you begin. Sex scenes aren't essential in a romantic novel, but love scenes are. The two shouldn't be confused, but you shouldn't even contemplate writing a romance without love scenes. How can any romance exist without them?

Whether the love scene is the more sweet and ethereal kind, or steamy enough to bring you out in a heat rash, depends to a large extent on the characters you've created. If they're very strong-willed and passionate people, it would be out of character for them merely to shake hands at the door every night.

'Whether the love scene is the more sweet and ethereal kind, or steamy enough to bring you out in a heat rash, depends to a large extent on the characters you've created.'

Need2Know

They must be portrayed as caring people, capable of loving one another - and remember that the reader wants to feel that sense of satisfaction when her hero and heroine go into their romantic clinch. Make no mistake about that! She'd be choosing a western if she wanted tough action.

Q. What about erotica? Would you include this in romance sub-genres?

A. One of the dictionary definitions of erotica is that it is 'explicitly sexual literature or art'. This sums it up well, and certainly romantic novels have become far more explicitly frank over the years. This is not wholly an unhealthy trend, in my opinion, but the real question is: where do you draw the line? Sex and love go together, but often so do sex and violence, and you may feel that books in the erotic list come more into the second category than the first.

Erotica in fiction has been around for a very long time, and is unlikely to go away. It can be vastly entertaining, or it can be downright sleazy. Your view may be that writing explicit scenes that go far beyond what many see as good taste, is nearer to pornography than romance.

So it's up to you whether or not you want to write erotica - or even if you could. Like all kinds of specialised writing, a skill is involved, and not least is a definite need to forget your inhibitions.

The market for erotica is strong at present. If it's hyped enough, it will probably continue to be. But how long the trend will last is anybody's guess. Before you even attempt to write for this market, my advice would be most definitely to send for any publisher's guidelines available, and also to read some of the books. They won't be to everyone's taste, but neither is sweet romance.

Q. Is there any difference between the terms 'romantic fiction' and 'a romance'? How would you define them?

A. This is a question that confuses many people. Logically, any novel in which a love story is featured could be called romantic fiction or a romance. But publishers have stronger feelings about this, and novels in any publisher's list have to be put into a category to be marketed.

'Romantic fiction' is generally applied to a far wider range of novels than 'a romance', and various sub-genres are described in a later chapter. A romance is generally a shorter novel written within certain guidelines issued by a publisher. The archetypal example of this is work published by Harlequin Mills & Boon.

The beginner might think that writing to a so-called formula is tedious and restricting, but there is tremendous scope within the guidelines, where each author can show ingenuity and develop an individual voice.

The central storyline of what is more generally termed 'romantic fiction' may be far more ambitious than in a straightforward romance. The novels are also much longer, resulting in what would be termed a 'fat book'.

I would stress that many of the ingredients of good fiction writing apply equally well to romantic fiction and romances, and to all other genres.

Q. Do you always have to think up your characters first?

A. You've touched on a point that confuses a lot of people. I always advise beginners to do so, because characterisation is so often their downfall. The characters don't spring to life off the page, and the novel is doomed to failure. And there's nothing more depressing than to be told that your characters are wooden. This failing can be helped enormously by doing the character sketch I mentioned earlier.

When you have more confidence in yourself as a romantic novelist, it can be easier to think of the background first, since the background will tend to dictate the way the characters behave and live. For instance, a glossy magazine office in New York will instantly bring to mind a certain set of characters that differ from those you would put into a cottage in the Scottish Highlands. Conversely, if you transposed each set of characters from their expected setting, you'd have two different novels, and this can often work very well.

I always have some idea of the background from the outset. If I know that my novel is going to be a romance, then the basics require a young, attractive heroine, and a strong, slightly older hero. There *may* be another woman to confuse the issue. There *may* be one or two other attractive men, but none who will take away the charisma of the hero.

These over-used stock characters are not so necessary nowadays, when outside influences can be the stumbling block to the romance rather than the sometimes boring foursome that develops. Or it can come from more interesting inner conflicts, arising from some internal turmoil in the heroine or hero's make-up.

Heroines these days are also far removed from the gentle, hero-dependent heroines of yesteryear. They can have high management positions, head a company, be daredevil airline pilots, or dedicated to environmental issues.

The conflicts between hero and heroine can be of a far more competitive nature than the constant irritations caused by misunderstandings with the Other Man or Woman.

The above comments refer especially to romances. In romantic fiction, since we've already differentiated between the sub-genres, characters can be far more diverse in age, ambition and so on. But in all cases, originality is what you should be aiming for, and you stand far more chance of publication if you create interesting and original characters.

Q. I'm not convinced that the background is more important than the characters. Convince me!

A. I didn't say it was more important. Ideally, in constructing a romantic novel, each should complement the other. For the reader, the characters are all-important, and she shouldn't even be aware that the background has played such a key role in producing this book for her enjoyment.

You as an author must see that the setting for your characters helps make your book different from someone else's. If I suggested the same main character to fifty people and asked them to give me the idea for a romance novel, I'd have fifty different stories, and each would be different because of the location - and the interpretation the author put on the given character.

Imagine that the heroine is a photographer. Now ask yourself the usual questions about her. Is she a society photographer? An animal photographer? A newspaper photographer? One who specialises in wedding photography? Or babies? Or in underwater photography? There are many more ideas. Each answer would put the girl into a different setting for a novel, meeting a different set of characters.

Q. I'm convinced! Where do you get your ideas?

A. Ideas are everywhere. Look through the pages of any magazine, at the adverts, the photographs, the problem pages. Read the newspapers and start your own collection of cuttings from any interesting stories that appeal to you. Collect travel brochures, catalogues from stately homes you have visited, theatre programmes, and use any information you can get to give you a starting point. A novel is a bit like a jigsaw. Many pieces go into it, and they all have to fit together, even though it seems impossible at first. Never go anywhere without a notebook to jot down that sudden burst of inspiration as you travel to work on train or bus. If you don't write it down at once, you may never find it again.

Q. I've thought of an idea for a romantic novel. Where do I go from there?

'Ideas are everywhere. Look through the pages of any magazine, at the adverts, the photographs, the problem pages.'

A. Great! But an idea is just an idea. It has to be nurtured like a tender seed until it grows into a full-blown plot. Don't rush in unless you're so bowled over by your idea that you can't wait to get pen to paper. If that's the case, then go ahead and write it, because you'll probably never recapture that lovely spontaneity again. Just be prepared to do as much revision as is required later!

A better way is not even to attempt to start your novel - except in your head - until you know you have sufficient material to sustain its length. Particularly in the case of a historical novel, which may have many twists and turns and changes of location, and a host of characters. I must admit that I've written novels at white-heat, and enjoyed it thoroughly, but for historicals I make endless notes before I begin, mulling over the ideas for some time, and then I make a rough synopsis.

Q. Help! Synopses frighten me. How do you write them and how do you know what's going to happen a few hundred pages further on?

A. A synopsis is no more than a guide as you're writing your novel. Writing a book without one is like embarking on a railway journey without knowing your destination. Yet many authors don't use them. I've written novels without a synopsis, but I defy any author to say that a good deal of thought and planning hadn't already gone on in their heads before they began. Much of the 'writing' of a novel is done before you ever sit down to a notebook or typewriter, often subconsciously.

But to get back to the mechanics of the synopsis. We'll say that you know the scene where your novel will begin and where it will end. Number a page with the approximate number of chapters, say one to twelve for a short novel. Against number one write your opening chapter scenes, against number twelve the closing chapter scenes.

Any novel needs to have pace and balance. It climbs steadily towards the climax at the end, with small peaks and troughs throughout. By the time you begin to think about your synopsis, you will have already decided on your characters, and probably have a rough idea of the conflicts and situations you're going to put them in. You'll already be farther ahead than you think you are, if your imagination has been stirred.

To balance your story, begin to fill in the other numbers between one and twelve with suggested scenes. You may decide to alternate a dramatic chapter with one of less frenzy, to give the reader a breathing space while still steadily building up the tension towards the conclusion. This is the very simplest way of creating a synopsis.

Q. Is that what you do?

A. I did it this way at first. Now what I do is simply write the lengthiest paragraph I can outlining the plot. Then I build on that, making each snippet into a separate paragraph, until the whole thing runs into pages. It takes me some time to construct a synopsis, but I must emphasise that you don't have to stick to it rigidly. It's your story, and you can change it at will, or when the characters dictate. That's a good moment, because then you know it's truly 'their story'.

Sometimes editors will commission a novel on a synopsis and one or more chapters. Even this needn't frighten you. All the editor wants to know is if you have the staying power to fulfil the promise of the early chapters, and if you're competent enough to understand the construction of a romantic novel. If you want to change the storyline as you write the book, it doesn't matter, providing the changes don't produce an entirely different book from the one the editor is expecting to see!

Q. I want to start with a contemporary romance with a local background - I've been told you should write about what you know. I'd like to write historicals one day though. How difficult is research?

A. If we all wrote only about what we know, there would be no historicals ever written, no romances set in exotic locations where the author has never set foot, no fascinating details of exciting lifestyles. Research is as necessary to the contemporary romantic novel as to the historical.

Some will say they never do any research and invent their backgrounds, and an example is the Scottish island I used in *Ashton's Folly*. This was totally fictitious, but it was endowed with all the physical characteristics of such an island. I was helped by memories of past holiday visits to the west coast of Scotland, and by studying maps to create the geographical location for my island of Maigh, which was to be off the mainland near Oban.

I obtained current train times between Bristol and Oban by writing to the rail company's publicity department for any relevant information. It was painless and simple research, but it all helped to make my novel read as authentically as if my island really existed. For me, of course, it did.

Research for historical romances deserves more space, and will be dealt with in chapter 9. A further book, *How to Research Your Novel,* by Jean Saunders, is also available in the Allison & Busby Writers' Guides series.

Q. I've heard about something called a 'flashback', but I haven't any idea what it means.

A. It is the term that authors use when it's necessary to tell the reader about something that happened before the present story or scene actually began.

They are best kept short, so that the progression of the novel is not held up for too long. They can occur anywhere within the book, and are especially useful in a contemporary novel, for instance, in explaining a character's reasons for his or her present behaviour.

Flashbacks can be included most smoothly by means of dialogue, so that one character tells another about past happenings, and this is the simplest way of writing them. Sometimes an author will convey a flashback by presenting a character in a reflective mood, thinking over something that happened in the past. Remembered dialogue can also occur in such a scene. In that case, you will find the need to use that most awkward of grammatical terms, the pluperfect tense.

Use it sparingly - once only if possible. Nothing is more irritating than to have several pages of 'had hads' to read. When it has been used, once or perhaps twice, the reader will quickly understand that the immediate scene is in flashback. If you can avoid it altogether, so much the better, but it is very often necessary to clarify a character's present mood.

A flashback which does not strictly deserve the name but is a useful device, is where an author begins a chapter with a paragraph or two of background information, such as the lead-up to a battle strategy in a historical novel.

This method should involve the fictional characters as quickly as possible, by bringing them into the battle/discussion/action, so that the page doesn't read like a list of statistics gleaned from the library!

By analysing published novels with all this in mind, the use of flashback will become clearer.

Q. I've followed all the instructions and written Chapter One at the top of the page. Despite knowing my characters and their background, my mind's suddenly gone blank. What now?

A. Now you're ready to begin.

Summing up

- Who? Where? Why? What? How?
- Write the book that appeals to you, not just one for the commercial market.
- Finding ideas. They're everywhere if you open your mind to possibilities.
- Synopses clarify your mind. Flashbacks help to fill in your characters' reasons for being in your book.

Chapter Three

Chapter One

Always begin your novel with an important scene. A contemporary romantic novel almost always begins at a moment of change in the heroine's life, but many of the points discussed here apply to both contemporary and historical romances.

Whether you like to start with a dramatic line of dialogue or to set the scene with a brief piece of vivid description is entirely up to you. But that first page *must* be an enticement to the reader to read on, to turn the page and find out what comes next.

It pays to spend plenty of time over that first page. Think of it as your window to a wonderful Aladdin's Cave within.

Unless that window is bright and attractive enough to lure the customer inside, she'll never know what delights she may be missing. And don't say to yourself that it will warm up later on - your book has to grab your reader on page one, or she may never get to 'later on'. A romantic novel plunges into the situation as quickly as possible, so that the reader knows what it's all about. A slow, ponderous beginning is old-fashioned. Today's readers live in a fast-paced world, and romantic novels reflect that world. That means introducing your characters as soon as possible, especially your heroine. Introduce her on the first page. The hero may not come into the story quite as quickly because we must have time to get to know a little about the heroine, and to throw too many characters in at once dilutes the impact of the central one.

Unless, of course, you've thought up some clever confrontation to begin your novel in which the two of them can be on stage from the start; then that's fine. In any case, the hero, or some pertinent reference to the hero and his role in the story, should certainly appear in the first few pages, and the problems the couple are going to experience be made quite clear by the end of chapter one.

'Always begin your novel with an important scene. A contemporary romantic novel almost always begins at a moment of change in the heroine's life.'

The resolution will be far from clear at this point, or there will be no story left to tell, but the difficulties the couple will encounter must be made interesting and intriguing to the reader. If the novel contains little more than scene after scene with the two of them arguing and bickering or with the heroine alternately fighting off the hero's advances or welcoming them, then the plot will be non-existent and the story will quickly become tedious.

Yet to produce a novel with substance and realism that is primarily about the developing romance between these two, you may wonder what is the point of bringing in more characters? The key here is never to introduce any character who doesn't have something to offer the story.

To bring in an interesting Spanish waiter just because you've just been on holiday to Majorca and remember the hotel waiter there with flashing dark eyes and a sexy smile, when all he does in your book is serve the white wine at dinner one evening, is not sufficient. To go into cosy and detailed descriptions of an entire family in pages and pages of retrospect, because you've been told that your heroine can't live in a void and must have a family background, when no member of that family has anything to do with the ever-present timing of your novel, is just padding.

You have two *main* characters in your book, the heroine and hero. She must be warm and attractive enough for the reader to like and identify with, and to hope fervently that she gets her man, and the hero . . . ah, the hero …

Who's the one person in the book that your reader is going to fall in love with? Who's the character who must stand head and shoulders above the rest, physically and mentally and dynamically? The hero, of course! He's the one who gets her sighing/drooling/etc, etc, so your hero *must* be absolutely the most attractive man you've ever described. Of *course* the reader wants to fall in love with him and to envy the heroine her luck, and of course you, the author, will fall in love with him too. If you know him well enough, you will.

But to calm down a little . . . Other characters have their roles to play too, and it's worth going into those roles before you rush into chapter one, because one or other of them is going to turn up quite soon in your novel.

Show and tell

Imagine that your contemporary novel begins with the heroine packing to leave home for a new job. You could describe the scene in several pages but they would be flat pages full of prose, and the only apprehension in the heroine's mind would come through her own thoughts.

You would be *telling,* not *showing.* There would be no excitement at the start of the novel, and beginning a romance should always be as exciting to the author as it is to the reader. Even if you have worked out a fairly detailed synopsis, your story should be exciting to you. Otherwise, discard it and try again.

At the beginning of the story just described, instead of letting her go into introspection to explain everything to the reader, give your heroine a flatmate, who is concerned about whether the heroine is doing the right thing or not - or perhaps envying her this great chance. And make your opening scene the dialogue between them, perhaps interspersed with little flashes of background explaining how the heroine came to this point in her life. Then the whole chapter will come alive from the first scene on page one.

Remember to use only *little* flashes of background here. You don't want to give away everything in the first chapter, or you'll have nothing left to say for the rest of the book. It's far better to filter in bits of information about the heroine; show her frame of mind when the book opens and what has led her up to the point where the book begins, rather than serving up great chunks of information all at once.

A romantic novel should give an illusion of reality. It should reflect real life; while glamorising it to a certain extent. In your own life, think back to the last interesting man you met at a party or social occasion. You didn't learn everything about him all at once. You got to know him gradually, because of the selected information he chose to give you about himself. And didn't that make him more interesting - more intriguing? You had that delicious guessing game with yourself, wondering about him. The same rule should be followed in fiction.

Of course, you could have learned a little more by overhearing some conversation about him. Or hearing how he responded to some sexy young woman, or older lady, or business acquaintance. Any of these could colour

'A romantic novel should give an illusion of reality. It should reflect real life; while glamorising it to a certain extent.'

your earlier reaction to this man. We all react differently to different people. We all put up our own defence barriers for various reasons. Put this into practise when you create the fictional characters for your romance.

Let's get back to the first page of our imaginary first chapter, with the heroine and her flatmate.

The flatmate is the minor character - the confidante - but through her we can give a sense of the heroine's looks, manner, voice, temperament, and learn a great deal more about her without writing an entire page of direct description.

The author would undoubtedly go into all these things in more detail at some other stage of the novel, but by using *indirect description* she will put across the initial information far more smoothly and effortlessly. The following illustration will show you exactly what I mean.

The flat looked as if a hurricane had blown through it, as Janet's normal tidiness was forgotten in the fever of packing.
'What do you really know about this man, Janet?' Ann said yet again.

'Any ad as glowing as the one you answered is bound to be suspect! I hope you're not being taken in by the glamour of working for a celebrity. It's not like you to be gullible.'

Janet flashed her a silencing look. Ann knew just how those vivid green eyes could quell anyone, but she doubted that the temperamental racing driver, Luke Peters, would think twice before he crossed her.

'You know as much as I do,' Janet retorted crisply, as though she was ticking off the items on a shopping list. 'I answered the ad. I was interviewed by the agent, since Luke Peters was in Monte Carlo at the time, and I was accepted. And I'm old enough to know what I'm doing, for heaven's sake!'

'Are you? You may be twenty-two and quite capable of holding down a top job as a private secretary, but the computer business is slightly different from following a racing driver around the world!' Ann answered her in the same defiant way.

Janet laughed. Ann had been her close friend for too long to feel real anger, and this was no time to begin a quarrel.

'You make it sound as if I'm to be his chief groupie!'

'Mind that you're not!' Ann warned. 'With your looks, you could be anything you liked, and Luke Peters is well known for his liking for brunettes. It wouldn't surprise me if that was half the reason the agent hired you on the spot.'

'So you think my secretarial references had nothing to do with it then?' Janet grinned.

Ann sighed. 'If I had legs like yours and a face and figure half as good, I wouldn't waste it on a racing driver I hadn't even met yet, no matter how good-looking!'

'I know all I need to know. He needs a promotions girl who doesn't mind travelling about, and he's paying me a good salary! I've seen Luke Peters on enough TV interviews recently to know the kind of man he is, and it doesn't frighten me off. I agree, though - he's not bad-looking!'

Ann was forced to laugh at the understatement. She gave up arguing and watched enviously as Janet continued packing her suitcase with the elegant clothes she always wore.

'Well, you've got more courage than me. I couldn't throw up the security of the last three years and go off into the unknown, just because I was getting into a rut and the boss was becoming a nuisance!'

'That was another little problem,' Janet agreed dryly, pausing in her packing for a moment. 'Look, don't worry about me, love, I'll keep in touch and tell you everything that happens - well, almost everything!'

In that opening scene, the reader has already discovered a great deal, not only about Janet, but about the hero as well. Beginning a novel in such a way brings the main characters and situation immediately into focus.

Ann, the minor character, is such an important part of Janet's background that she can logically reappear at intervals throughout the book.

She has already served a purpose in telling the reader of the approaching change in Janet's life, something about her appearance, and the reasons for leaving her present employment. The reader knows how attractive Janet is, and that her new employer may not be the easiest of men to deal with, since the hint that he's a bit of a womaniser is already planted in the reader's mind.

The conflict in this novel will clearly involve the temperaments of the two main characters. Where Ann can be useful in future chapters is in telephone conversations with Janet, having things confided to her in letters, providing a shoulder to weep on when things go wrong, as they inevitably will.

The flatmate can be the trusting ear into which the heroine can betray all the emotions she is keeping from the hero.

In a historical romance, the substitute for the flatmate is often the understanding aunt or old retainer, or the faithful little maid to whom the heroine can tell everything, knowing it will never go beyond the four walls of her bedroom. Even a historical heroine's pet or the horse she rides in a fury, can be used as a minor character, 'listening' as she pours out her frustrations aloud, knowing there's no danger of her anguished words being repeated.

Variations on these characters will appear again and again in published novels. Use them with caution, but take every advantage of them. Don't overdo them, but don't disregard their usefulness either.

Keeping the hero on stage at all times is often a major headache to the first-time romantic author. If you refer back to the illustration of the first scene in chapter one, he has already been described briefly. Once the working relationship between hero and heroine begins, then inevitably, because this is a romance, something more must spark between them.

The hero is a racing driver, which points to tension and drama in his life in the way he lives hard and plays hard, and in clashes between them when the heroine begins to resent his attentions. As she begins to fall in love with him, the more she hates the dangers of his career, and the hangers-on on its periphery. There's plenty of scope here for skirmishes that aren't contrived.

But he can't and shouldn't be around her every minute of the time. This is when *indirect presence* plays a big part in the novel. The heroine could be startled by his appearance on a television news programme when she wasn't expecting it. She could hear his voice on the telephone, and suddenly realise how seductive it can be when he's not censuring her.

She could study his newspaper cutting, old photographs when he was much younger, new photographs with some beautiful girl that arouses jealousy in her mind to take her by surprise. Or a candid photo of herself and the hero caught by a newspaper photographer and linking their names together romantically, which could make her realise that she wishes the inferences were true!

These are just some of the techniques whereby the heroine can describe the hero's appearance in her thoughts, and portray her feelings towards him at that moment. If your imagination has been stimulated so far, then you should already be inventing more ideas for yourself.

Summing Up

- The important first page - the window on a new world for your readers.

- Show, don't tell.

- Filter in the background gradually, rather than with great chunks of research information.

- Direct and indirect descriptions help to vary your writing.

Chapter Four
Believable Characters

Viewpoint

Many beginners think it's easier to write in the first person, and if you find it difficult to identify with your characters, then that's probably true. But apart from the fact that many publishers of romantic novels don't like first-person narratives, there are technical drawbacks that may not be immediately apparent.

If you tell your heroine's story in the first person, then everything that occurs in the novel must be seen, heard, experienced through her eyes and ears alone and it narrows the freedom of your imagination. Also, there is sometimes a cosy feel to the first-person narrative, a sense of the eternal 'I' being a little God-like in telling the tale.

All this is more easily avoided in the third-person narrative. It's as if the author can stand back and be more of an observer as she guides her fictional characters through their romance.

In a contemporary romance, although one viewpoint throughout the book is generally accepted as the norm, there is a trend towards the hero taking over the viewpoint for short scenes, but certainly not for the entire novel. This does help in conveying his feelings and emotions more precisely. But, for the beginner, I would strongly advise keeping to the heroine's viewpoint in the third person.

Historical novels are slightly different. I've written them from first and third-person viewpoints, and also from multiple viewpoints (that is, getting into the mind of the character who will give most impact to a particular scene).

Experienced authors of historical romance will change viewpoint within a chapter, but it's a technique that needs to be handled skilfully and smoothly, and studying the work of such authors will best show how it's done.

Always, if you do risk changing viewpoint within a chapter in a historical romance, put a blank double-line space, so that the reader gets a chance to catch her breath and knows in advance that there's about to be a scene change.

If it's done well, it works superbly.

Names

There are fashions in names as in everything else. Victorians wouldn't recognise a Wayne or a Gary, for instance, since they're far too modern. Haven't you heard of children christened Elvis, who possibly cringe in later life at the association? It's a mistake to have anything with too pointed an association when the name is unusual.

Conversely, some names never lose their popularity. Names of royalty are fairly perpetual, and biblical names have a strangely authentic ring to them when used in a historical romance.

The name of a character is more than just a label. It immediately brings a certain type to mind, whether we like it or not. Jim or James and Jamie conjure up quite different associations. Elizabeth might have more dignity than Liz, but Liz might be more suitable for a young, contemporary heroine who's a bit scatty.

I start a 'cast list' for every new novel. I may have decided on only two names at first, the hero and heroine. Beside each one I write my character sketch, and as any new character comes into the book, I add them to the list.

Try to avoid a romantic heroine a gimmicky name, and this applies to the hero too. A while ago it was all the rage to give him a very virile-sounding name like Teak, and Other Man a weaker name like Bobby. (With apologies to all the Bobbies . . .) You may like Teak. You may only feel an empathy with your dashing hero if you label him thus. That's fine. But I still think it's a bit gimmicky, and it might make some readers wince.

I choose strong but feminine names for my heroines, which reflects the way I think of them. In historical novels I've used Loveday, Katrina, Julia, Rosie, Roslyn, Morwen, Briony, among others. Historical heroes too, must be strong, but not weird. Mine have been Adam, Will, Robert, Justin, Maxwell, Dominic . . .

'There are fashions in names as in everything else. Victorians wouldn't recognise a Wayne or a Gary, for instance, since they're far too modern.'

I still recall my Dominic with a special glow. Now there was a hero . . . But naturally, choosing names is a personal thing, and you'll disagree with some of my choices. Which is just as well. Otherwise, every romantic novel that was published would have the same two characters, wouldn't they?

Characterisation – Appearance

Having dealt with the subject of names, how else do we define our characters, making them indelible in the reader's mind so that they linger there long after the book is put down? Try to get a quick mental picture of someone you know, whom you haven't seen for a while. What do you recall most vividly? The smile, the walk, the voice.

The number of times a smile has been described in romantic novels is endless. But doesn't a face change when a smile lights it up, or twists it derisively, or hides some sadness? A smile can express some facet of a character in an instant. Smiles can be tender or wide, radiant or non-existent, downright ugly or leering.

The way a person moves can be used very successfully to reveal the mood of a character, needing little more description. When the hero strides across the room, or covers it in two long paces, you already know he's tall and powerful and probably in a bad temper. You don't need to spell it out any more clearly to the reader. Avoid if you can the loping walk, the tigerish prowl, the barking laugh, in fact anything with an animal connotation. The dark curling mat of hair on the hero's chest has also become a pretty boring cliché. Yes, many readers like hairy-chested heroes. But why does he have to have a mat of it? He sounds more like a hearthrug than a man.

The heroine, of course, always moves gracefully. In a historical romance, the elegance of floating, ankle-length gowns and flowing cloaks lends so much to the romantic aura you're trying to create. So do the fabulous jewels and costly robes worn by courtesans.

Denim jeans don't ever sound quite the same, but if that's what your contemporary heroine would be wearing, then it's up to you to make her seem as attractive as possible in your description of the way they fit her skin and emphasise her femininity.

Characterisation – Voice

Fictional characters don't really come alive until you hear them speak. I once heard an actress say that she has to get the feet right before she can play a part properly. In a novel I have to get the character's voice right, and it always starts with my heroine. I need to know her voice, to hear the nuances in whatever accent I'm giving her, and I 'listen' to her as I write her lines of dialogue. All the descriptions in the world about rosebud lips and flaxen hair don't let you know your heroine half as much as providing her with the right voice for her character, in the right pitch and accent, and knowing how that voice would change in certain situations and when addressing different people. In many unpublished manuscripts (which will probably remain unpublished), the most glaring fault is the woodenness of the dialogue. If only the author would get to know her characters properly, the dialogue would almost begin to dictate itself.

Don't be so busy making sure that the heroine follows the approved pattern, that eyes are china blue and nose tip-tilted or, in the hero's case, aquiline (which sounds equally peculiar to me), that the physical appearance dominates all else.

What will emerge are characters that are beautiful plastic clones of those in every other romantic novel. The reader may be able to see the heroine clearly from your description, but she'll have no more substance than the picture on a chocolate box. She won't be real if all you have given the reader is little more than a photograph.

Don't forget to give your characters warmth. Readers want to care what happens to your characters, and particularly the heroine. They want to laugh when she laughs, cry when she cries and vicariously enjoy her love scenes. They want to share her excitement, and to feel a sense of pleasure and satisfaction when she reaches her happy ending.

How can the reader do that if something as basic as the expression in the heroine's voice never varies, whether she is speaking to the milkman or the bus driver or the man she's supposed to love so passionately? Not only does the tone of a person's voice change in conversation with different people but so does the choice of words used. A character quickly becomes cardboard if the author ignores this point.

You may already have discovered how frustrating it can be when you're trying to write dialogue between your characters and it won't come right. No matter how much you revise and revise, the scene still doesn't work.

At this point you think your plot is hopeless. You're convinced you're a failure and you're certain you'll never write another word. You're not alone, dear aspiring author! Everyone goes through it, and that feeling doesn't end with writing the first book.

But in reality that moment shouldn't be thought of as failure, hard as it may seem to you. Because you have reached that magical, perceptive moment when your characters have become so real to you that you know instinctively when you're putting the wrong words into their mouths. You're listening to them in your subconscious, and they're telling you that the cold print you're dictating for them is not the way they would react in that particular situation.

Although the author must always remain in control, don't you think there's a kind of magic in breathing such life into your imaginary people? Until now they existed only in your head and no one else's. It can be a wonderful moment when a reader says how much she loved a particular heroine, or fell for your gorgeous hero, because then you know that they were as real for the reader as they became for you.

Baring the Emotions

By the very nature of the genre, the characters in romantic novels should have deep, explosive emotions, and you should let them show these emotions where necessary. My heroine is always fiery but vulnerable, always a strong-willed young lady who is still capable of showing that she can be gentle and feminine. Each one is different in other ways, but those are qualities I like to give her.

This applies whether I'm writing a contemporary or a historical romance. And since I want my reader to fall in love with my hero, he has to be charismatic too. And as I don't want my heroine to end up being strident and overbearing, the hero has to be the strongest character in the book. But he doesn't have to be portrayed as perfect in every way.

If your main characters are too idealised, there would be no story to tell. No conflict would arise, and conflict provides the vitality and staying power of any novel in any category. Both hero and heroine will have some flaws, and it's imperative to let the reader in on them, although the hero and heroine can, and probably will, be unaware of each other's hang-ups, which only adds to the frustration and conflict between them.

This is where the confidante character mentioned in chapter 3 can be invaluable. Through the confidante the reader can learn what the problem is and how it arose. Knowing this, she will sympathise, understand and forgive. She'll be even more anxious for the story to be resolved happily, and she'll really care about those characters.

'If your main characters are too idealised, there would be no story to tell. No conflict would arise, and conflict provides the vitality and staying power of any novel in any category.'

If it seems as if romantic novels are all about drama and tension and conflict, you may wonder if there's any room for humour in them. Definitely yes, if the humour comes through witty but not cruel dialogue, if a heroine is endearingly scatty but not dim, if a pet such as a lumbering dog upsets a picnic or smothers an elegant hero in mud at the most inopportune moment.

In small doses, humour can give an added dimension to your characters, but never lose sight of the fact that you're writing a romantic novel, not a farce. If your characters' laughter can develop into tenderness or even tears (usually the heroine's, not the hero's!) then so much the better.

Having got this far, don't spoil it all by relying on contrivances in the plot, or letting a hero who was self-assured and aloof throughout the novel suddenly confess on the final page that he loved the heroine all the time, without giving the reader any indication until then of a change of heart!

Make your characters consistent - and do make sure to convey to your readers that the hero is falling in love too, with all the complexities that can bring. Love is not an exclusively female emotion. Wouldn't it be boring if it was?

Summing Up

- Make sure their names fit their personalities, whether contemporary or historical.
- Get to know them as friends and not just as puppets.
- Make each one an individual and easily recognisable by readers.
- Give them faults and virtues, hopes and ambitions.
- The hero is falling in love too!

Chapter Five

The Language of Love

In order to 'listen' to the characters speak, the author must give them lines of dialogue to say. Obvious, isn't it? Yes it's amazing how many beginners avoid dialogue. They will write pages and pages of flowery description and ponderous flashbacks, and long before anything of real importance has begun to happen, the reader's attention has started to wander.

It's often true that one good crisp page of sparkling dialogue in a romantic novel can reveal more about character and plot than several pages of dense prose.

'Ah ha!' thinks the wily beginner. 'But I can fill the required pages of my novel with half the effort if two pages of prose can take the place of one of dialogue!' Wrong. The result will be an essay, a report, a flat descriptive piece. And no matter how colourful, it will be without that essence of vitality that dialogue brings. An editor will take one look at those dark pages and scream: 'Padding!' And if the rest of the manuscript follows the same trail, it will probably be smartly returned to the author with a rejection slip.

Dialogue brings life to books and to people. How dreary everyday life would be if we all went about silently, with no communication between us. That's exactly the effect of a romantic novel without conversation between the characters.

I can hear you all muttering that of course you would put dialogue into your novel. But one manuscript that I was asked to criticise ran for the first fifty pages without one word of it. The author had thought up every possible means of getting round the problem, until it became a kind of private game between me and the manuscript to spot the devices. When some characters finally spoke, it was little more than such scintillating comments as:

> 'In order to 'listen' to the characters speak, the author must give them lines of dialogue to say.'

- 'Hello.'

- 'Pass the salt, please.'

- 'Nice morning, isn't it?'

- 'What are we going to do today?'

Yes, we would use any of these remarks in everyday life. Yes, you may have seen similar ones in many another romantic novel, but not just as cold, trite little phrases to vary the look of the printed page. Any of those phrases, used to describe the mood of the person at that moment, with qualifying adverbs, may be perfectly acceptable, but to think that as they are they provide the kind of dialogue needed in a romantic novel is ludicrous.

We have a beautiful language, and we must exploit it to the full to convey exactly what we want our character to express. We have beautiful words and phrases that can immediately conjure up images in our minds, so why settle for anything more mundane?

'The purpose of dialogue in fiction is more complex than the average reader might think.'

Remember, too, that similar words have subtly different meanings. Words such as 'sweetly', 'gently' and 'tenderly' don't give exactly the same meaning to the reader. If any author can't hear the difference in her head, she should practise saying the dialogue aloud to understand the precise meaning she's trying to convey.

Use of a thesaurus will undoubtedly help, but knowing the subtleties of your own language is even better. Know your characters too, because then you sense exactly what they are trying to say.

Purposes of fictional dialogue

The purpose of dialogue in fiction is more complex than the average reader might think. It moves the story along, it shows the reader what's happening by verbal involvement of the characters, rather than merely telling it through the narration of the author.

Dialogue reveals character. By the interaction of two characters talking, the reader can be told what happened before the story began in a painless and smooth manner. It can show the character's mood at the time of the conversation (as was illustrated in the chapter dealing with the opening scene, but I think it's a point worth repeating). Make full use of it.

Don't state in your novel that your character had a sarcastic wit, or that your heroine made the hero laugh by her bubbling excitement, unless you back it up by their discussion.

The reader wants to *hear* that biting wit, and decide for herself whether the hero is a clever intellectual or trying to goad the heroine into a response for his own reasons. She wants to be as involved in the hero's reactions to the heroine's excitement as if it's happening to her.

The character sketch that you've already created in your mind's eye - you have, haven't you? - will let you see how excitement makes her face glow; makes his mouth tighten or twist with mockery. You'll know how the heroine feels when their eyes meet - yes, across a crowded room, if you like! - and you'll share in that moment if you've visualised them fully.

The voices you've given them will make the words they say the only ones possible at that particular time, in those particular circumstances. That's true identification with your characters.

All the ingredients that go into the making of a romantic novel inevitably overlap, in characterisation and dialogue especially, because each complements and is a part of the other.

If you have been creating your characters with sufficient thought, you'll have given them motivation for all their actions. You'll have avoided stereotyping them. You won't have portrayed every female newspaper reporter as hard-boiled, smoking endless cigarettes with fingernails like red talons, for instance, as was once beloved of magazines.

Know what your character *does,* and *why* and *how* she does it. Know what she *says,* and *why* and *how* she says it.

The great advantage that human beings have over other animals is the capacity for speech. No two people speak exactly alike. Imagine your characters' dialogue as if it's a radio play where actors have to rely solely on sound variations in the voice and individual speech mannerisms. The written story should have just as much impact in its characterisation.

Showing the character's mood at the time of speaking has its own advantage in the written word. The use of adverbs - *he muttered angrily; she said lovingly.* Or the use of active verbs with the line of dialogue - *she breathed/smiled/ gloated/screamed.* The more you vary the ways of qualifying dialogue, the more interestingly and smoothly the story reads.

As long as the reader is quite sure who's speaking, it's often effective not to put anything at all, just the lines of dialogue. But don't overdo it. A whole page consisting of mere lines of dialogue will leave the reader totally confused. It has that back-and-forth effect that quickly becomes irritating and somehow loses any feeling of warmth between the characters. If you're trying to get just that effect, that's a different matter, but still go with caution. Once the reader has to work back to see who's saying what, you've lost her.

A comment at the beginning of the dialogue will often establish the character's mood:

> Her breath caught in her throat.

The line of dialogue immediately follows. The reader will know at once who's speaking, and that the character is feeling emotional or upset without your actually saying as much. Allow your reader to use her own imagination to become involved in the story. Don't give everything away, but always aim for clarity.

Falling in love

Two people in a romantic novel are going to fall in love. They may be strangers before the story begins. They may be old friends or mere acquaintances who suddenly discover something magical about each other. They may once have been lovers and are now divorced or separated.

Whatever the role the author has given them, they have to get to know each other in a new light. They have to discover new facets of one another that make each realise that they have now met the only person in the world with whom they want to share their life. This is a feeling that gradually becomes overwhelming. The author has to make the reader feel this too.

These two characters must live out their big scenes in a romantic novel, whether it's a blistering fight, a passionate love scene, or an emotional goodbye. The reader in a romance is in effect eavesdropping on many intimate moments. For a romance reader to get the emotional reaction you're seeking you must have it first. If you're succeeding in writing realistic dialogue, then you'll be smiling as you write the joyous parts of your novel. You'll have a tightness in your throat when you write the scenes where the lovers get together at last and go towards their happy ending, because it's what they - and you - have been leading towards throughout the pages of the novel. Everyone feels pleasure at reaching their happy ending.

Always make your dialogue consistent, not only with the characters you have created for your romance, but also with their locality, their status, their ages. Older people speak differently from teenagers in tempo and content, and speech patterns vary in different parts of the country.

The time for staccato dialogue and prose is when swift movement is required, at a time of panic or suspense. Terse, brief dialogue conveys fear with few spoken words, and this is when emotional reactions can be emphasised most of all, this time through the *thoughts* of the heroine in those turbulent moments.

The Gothic heroine who is in danger, or the sophisticated modern heroine suddenly frightened in unfamiliar rural surrounding, can react in such a way as to bring out unexpected tenderness in the toughest hero, and she can respond with an emotion that stuns her.

Neither situation would be contrived, providing your plot was sound and it was perfectly logical for the characters to be in the places you've put them at the given time. So much of successful romantic novel writing depends on logic. I try to keep that thought uppermost in my mind whenever I come to a tricky patch in my novels. *Write visually and think logically*, are my watchwords. Because the moment an editor reads a manuscript that has lost credibility, it's ready for rejection. And the most incredible thing of all is reaching the last couple of pages with the two of them declaring their undying love, when they've hardly spoken to one another for the rest of the book.

Distinctive characters

The way your contemporary characters speak to each other will be different from the way historical ones do.

If we don't *know* the kind of people we want to write about in contemporary novels, we can almost always find some television programme to illustrate them. We can listen to them on buses, at cinemas, at places of business, in our own homes. If your characters are going to be involved in the pop music world, for example, it's easy enough to listen to everyday slang, and to various speech idioms; listening to the radio will also help.

The way characters of another age addressed one another varies more strikingly according to their class and background. In a historical novel, the writing is often more robust, the characters needing to fend for themselves in desperate circumstances, and the language must reflect this.

The author shouldn't shy away from letting a hero use strong language if the situation merits it. If he's rescuing the heroine from danger, he'll undoubtedly shout and probably swear at his opponent. Don't be afraid to put the words into his mouth that such a protective hero would use. He'll only come across to the reader as too feeble to be given the name of hero if he acts primly in a violent situation. And don't be too coy in your love scenes. Dialogue expresses feelings and emotions, and you mustn't let yourself be inhibited at the thought of Great Aunt Ethel blushing at any written exhibition of love.

Characters in fiction are always a bit larger than life. Think of the memorable ones, the gorgeous ones. The Scarlet Pimpernel, Rhett Butler, Heathcliff . . . heroes all, and none of them skimpily drawn by their authors. Each was a well-rounded character, and each one had every woman reader falling in love with him. (Didn't you?)

In every kind of romantic novel, the written dialogue isn't *quite* normal speech, because of its fictional purpose, but it's still useful to follow some ordinary speech patterns.

In real life, people interrupt. This is effective in fiction as long as it's not overdone, when it becomes irritating. In a romance, it's very often a useful ploy, when perhaps the heroine starts to say something, then stops, realising she may be giving away too much, either about her feelings or motives.

In real life, people forget what they started to say. Useful again for a fictional character, either accidentally or deliberately. But do this with extra caution, or your young heroine may sound as if she's going senile.

Never let your dialogue become speeches. People don't normally go on at great length to each other, and neither should they in fiction. One of Shakespeare's heroes may have made dauntingly long speeches to his lady, but today's heroine would be turned off long before he reached the end of it, and be looking around for someone less verbal.

Keep the actual sentences of dialogue reasonably short, but keep them frequent. And let the exchanges between hero and heroine take up the larger proportion of the total dialogue in the novel. It's their story after all.

As for what they actually say to one another . . . well, you're the author.

'Never let your dialogue become speeches. People don't normally go on at great length to each other, and neither should they in fiction.'

Summing Up

- Characters must talk to one another.
- Make their dialogue realistic.
- Don't give them long speeches.
- Adapt it to the ages of your characters.
- Adapt it to their status in life.

Chapter Six
Appealing to the Senses

The romantic novel has been described as a celebration of the senses. This may be a statement to make the critics mock, but it's an undoubted fact that in a convincing romantic novel, all five recognised senses are very much involved, and probably a few more as well.

Sight, hearing, smell, taste, touch

Any one of them, and preferably a combination of two or more, can bring a person, a memory, an occasion, a mood, instantly to mind. Haven't we all proved it in real life at some time or another?

Whether you set your novel in the beautiful Highlands of Scotland, the dusty Australian outback, or on the fabulous desert plains of Tunisia, let your readers see, feel and taste the atmosphere. However homely or intimate or dramatic the scene, it can be brought instantly to life by using vivid and evocative words to appeal to the reader's senses.

Baking bread - doesn't that conjure up a delicious smell of steamy warmth? The tang of vinegar on humble fish and chips eaten out of newspaper - can't you taste them?

Can't you feel the nostalgia of yesterday when you describe the hot sand between your toes on a sun-baked beach, and that blissful walk along the water's edge to cool off? Visualise that lovely sunset as you describe it, see all the beautiful colours, and don't be afraid of the words.

The romantic novelist paints word pictures to bring all of these things to life, to make our readers see what we see in our imagination. We're in the nostalgia game, whether we like it or not.

'The romantic novelist paints word pictures to bring all of these things to life, to make our readers see what we see in our imagination. We're in the nostalgia game, whether we like it or not.'

Be careful not to get so carried away that what you write begins to sound ridiculous. Several short, emotive phrases of description will be far more effective than paragraph after paragraph all virtually saying the same thing. The most certain way to let your reader experience what your characters are experiencing is to appeal directly to their senses. Let's take them one at a time.

Sight

It doesn't take much imagination to let your characters see each other and the background where the novel takes place. Those are the obvious tangible ingredients of the novel. But let the characters dream a little too.

Let your heroine remember a very special evening spent with the hero. In letting her 'see' it all over again, your reader will sigh over the memory too.

Seeing specific objects that recall happier days, such as photographs, old letters, etc, has been mentioned earlier. Descriptions of court occasions, glittering jewels, gorgeous ballgowns, the colour of historical scenes, are a godsend to the author with a vivid imagination. Let your reader see and experience with your characters those magical or terrible times.

Don't balk at battle scenes. In *Scarlet Rebel* (Jean Saunders) I described my hero's gory involvement in the battle of Culloden with as much attention to detail as in the more romantic scenes in the book. Give each scene full measure.

Actual dream sequences in romantic novels can be a little tricky. They've been wildly overdone, but what device hasn't, in any novel you've ever read? There are only so many basic plots, so many situations. It's the interpretation each author puts on the scene that gives it freshness and vitality. A reader will forgive practically anything that's been done before, if the author gives it a fresh new look.

I've used the dream sequence in several of my romantic novels, contemporary and historical. There are two ways of leading into it. One is to guide the reader gently into the dream, through the heroine's inability to sleep, perhaps with the breeze throwing moonlit patterns on the bedcover and almost mesmerising her into a semi-hypnotised state. Smooth, effective, and usually ending with the heroine waking up in a tangle of bedclothes, after whatever form the dream takes.

Your choice of novel will dictate this. A Gothic romance will probably have a dream that verges on a nightmare, with the heroine uncertain which male character is villain or hero.

A contemporary romance may well have a more erotic dream sequence. A doctor/nurse romance may be more dramatic, with the heroine worrying about the hero's professional capabilities, naturally making full use of her sight of the hero's strong, capable, caring hands.

A historical dream sequence can go any way you want it to, from the full-blooded excitement of a Victorian girl being carried off in her lover's arms to the chaste first kiss she hasn't yet known, to the explicit sex scenes unacceptable for her to experience while she's awake, because of her upbringing and social background. It all depends which kind of novel you're writing, how light or deep your dream sequence will be.

The reader can 'see' all this, through the eyes of the heroine, but my advice must still be to use dream sequences with care. Their greatest use is in revealing the heroine's longings, however repressed they may be in her waking hours.

The second way of starting a dream sequence is by using it to begin a scene, so that the reader isn't immediately sure if it's really happening or not. Effective, but never prolong this type of scene, or the reader will feel cheated when she realises it's 'just a dream' and the real action hasn't yet begun.

Hearing

Self-explanatory, of course. To hear the hero's rich, deep voice is part of his charm to every romantic heroine. Did you ever read about a hero with a high-pitched whine? The hero must be authoritative and forceful, giving the impression that he's vastly capable of taking care of the heroine and the entire world if need be.

His voice can be heard in many circumstances, some of which were mentioned earlier. In close contact the voice will deepen, or it will whisper seductively, the breath will be warm against the timbre of the voice that will spark it off.

The telephone conversation can reveal something in his voice that she may not have recognised before. The TV or radio interview could reveal a different side to him. You'll see how everything that the author puts into a romantic novel is intended to flesh out these characters, to give them life and substance.

Sounds evoke memories. Music - a favourite song, or one that was playing when the lovers first met. Any love song that fills the heroine with emotion. Thundering hoofbeats. The rush of waves on a pebble beach. A train hurtling through the night. Christmas carols. The rich sound of an old accordion - don't you immediately think of Paris?

'Sounds evoke memories. Music - a favourite song, or one that was playing when the lovers first met.'

Smell

Perfume, naturally. Hers, that he gave her. His, in the form of aftershave. The scent of wild flowers. New-mown hay. Herbal shampoo. The damp rough-textured scent of wool after being caught in a shower. Earth after rain. Woodsmoke. The clean distinctive smell of writing paper. The strange, dense smell of ink. Full-blown roses. Mint. Wild strawberries. Mountain air. Old leather. An expensive cigar. Freshly ground coffee.

If some of the smells mentioned in the above paragraph have already reached your senses, then you'll see how brief a description is needed when the smell is an evocative one.

In one of my historical novels, a key male character died (obviously not the hero or the story would have ended right there!). His young wife, left with three small children, was naturally distraught. I conveyed her emotion very vividly by a poignant scene with little actual description.

When the heroine of the novel arrived to visit the young widow, it was to find her furiously ironing a pile of her dead husband's shirts that she had just washed, and then holding the warm shirt to her face, saying that the hot iron brought out the scent of his body, keeping him with her just a bit longer.

Taste

The taste of the hero's lips against the heroine's mouth, defining warmth and passion. Smoke so dense it can be tasted. Welcome rain in a parched throat. Any kind of food or drink that appeals to the senses, sizzling steak or pink champagne. The taste of fear. Salty air. The taste of a dust-storm.

The sense of taste is a very personal one, and one that the author can exploit in innumerable ways to enhance the characters' emotions and the attraction of setting in the novel. Especially when the use is a less usual one, as in the taste of snow as opposed to the way it feels on the skin.

Touch

This is surely the most important sense of all. Lovers constantly touch with fingertips, with their arms, embracing physically with their bodies, mentally with their eyes, their thoughts.

Two people who are falling in love want above all else to be touching one another. The need to be close, to feel the warmth of the other's body - whether in a horse-drawn carriage or a racing London taxi, in a crowded dancehall or the intimacy of a hotel bedroom - is fundamental to the characters in every romantic novel.

The first meeting, and the first touch between hero and heroine is all-important. Not only where and when it happens, but the way it's described, and the effect it has on each of them, especially the heroine.

The most fleeting touch of fingertip against cheek can be as evocative and sensual as the most explicit love scene. Some authors, such as those who write Regency historical romances, would say almost more so.

The authors of classical romantic novels could allow their lovers little more than a tender glance, a formal handshake or an occasional kiss on the back of the hand, but the sexual tension between them was as evident in those books as in today's more explicit ones.

The feel of objects presents the romantic author with a wealth of opportunities to bring the scene to life. The heroine's shimmering silk dress that rustles with every movement. The sensuality of velvet. The texture of the hero's slightly unshaven face. The coolness of 'his' face against 'hers' when he returns after a journey. Springy moorland turf. The feel of a cat's fur, lovely to some people, repellent to others. Birds' feathers. Falling petals. The smooth perfection of polished wood.

'What of the elusive sense - the so-called sixth sense? In a romantic suspense novel or a Gothic romance, the heroine will very often be expected to use her sixth sense - that almost occult awareness that something is wrong.'

I have listed the preceding phrases to show how you can think up ideas to use in your romantic novel. Once you begin to develop the receptive mind of the practised author, you see everyday things around you in a different way. Even things that are familiar to you.

If the old stone bridge that has spanned a stream for centuries in your own town could only speak, what a story it could tell. Why not imagine some of those stories? What kind of people have walked over that bridge? Rich, poor, lonely, happy?

That ancient oak tree that's been standing on the village green for so long that its roots are beginning to push through the turf. Would pretty Victorian girls have danced around the maypole beneath its shade, hoping to catch the eye of the squire's son? How many departing soldiers and their sweethearts have carved their initials on its gnarled trunk? Perhaps present-day hippies and their girlfriends have camped there overnight before being moved on.

Using the sixth sense

What of the elusive sense - the so-called sixth sense? In a romantic suspense novel or a Gothic romance, the heroine will very often be expected to use her sixth sense - that almost occult awareness that something is wrong.

In historical romances, the sixth sense crops up all the time, but rather less so in contemporaries. I fail to see why that should be. Do contemporary heroines have less of this slightly supernatural awareness? They shouldn't have, when feelings and emotions reputedly continue the same throughout the ages. Why not exploit this more in contemporary fiction?

The receptiveness that comes with practice to any author has played a part in my own writing career. I firmly believe in the subconscious continuing to work for us, even when we've put down the pen or left the typewriter, or switched off the word processor for the day.

Personal work methods are immaterial. What is important is that if we're enthusiastic and totally involved in our work, then the novel we're writing continues in our head, consciously or subconsciously. And facts that we didn't even realise we knew somehow emerge to be used in the next day's stint of writing - or have already been used!

I was halfway through writing my historical romance, *The Sweet Red Earth* (Rowena Summers). I wanted to find a name for a minor male character that wouldn't clash with the others, especially Adam, my hero. I'd just bought a new book of names and meanings and was browsing through when I discovered that Adam was Hebrew for 'red earth'.

I had no idea until that moment. Or had I? Had something deep in my subconscious told me? Was it an example of inherited memory that I'm convinced exists?

Naturally, I made sure that Adam found an opportunity to inform the heroine of this fact, since the red earth in the title was integral to the story.

Ideas for romantic novels are everywhere if we open our minds and let the ideas flow in. By applying all our own senses to what is around us, we're much more able to endow our fictional characters with human virtues and frailties, and perhaps a little extra besides.

By the simple method of letting your characters use the same five - or six - senses as ourselves, you will also be automatically adding one more essential ingredient to your romantic novel. You'll feel a special care for your characters and their journey between the covers of your book. You'll be writing from the heart. And it will show.

Summing Up

- Engage all the senses to enhance your writing.
- Use emotive words in your descriptions.
- Aim to let readers experience what the characters experience.
- Remember the elusive sixth sense.

Chapter Seven
Putting in the Steam

No romantic novel can be worthy of the name if it fails to include love scenes. And make no mistake about it, when a reader buys a paperback romance, or takes home a good meaty hardback from the library with that alluring picture of an embrace on the jacket, she's already anticipating a good sprinkling of love scenes.

If that wasn't the prime reason for her choice, she'd be picking out westerns or crime novels or science fiction. The author who can't fulfil this basic requirement doesn't stand a chance of being accepted by the publishers of romantic fiction, who know what their readers want and have plenty of other authors willing to give it to them.

Having said that, a romantic novel that is no more than a string of sex scenes put in merely to titillate the reader will fail. Without a good story to uphold them, love scenes can quickly become boring.

Planning and balancing the plot is extremely important, whether you make a detailed synopsis from the start, or let the story evolve as it will and revise and polish it later. Write your book whichever way suits you.

If the characters you've created are believable people involved in conflicts and situations that are logical and progressive, then your love scenes will grow out of the story, and out of the characters' lives and personalities. You won't have to insert a love scene every twenty pages or so because you think that's what an editor will expect to see.

But what about those love scenes? How to get your lovers into a clinch that doesn't sound cloying or slushy or almost pornographic - or so brisk and businesslike that you wonder how these two ever got within a mile of each other, let alone this wonderful close encounter.

'No romantic novel can be worthy of the name if it fails to include love scenes.'

First, it's a mistake to describe the physical actions of these two people as if they're mute. People do talk when they make love, however distractedly, and a page of flowery, euphoric description without a single word of dialogue is copping out.

That style was very popular until quite recently, but the emphasis has already shifted, and the breathless euphoria has given way to more warmth and tenderness between the characters, making them seem more like real people. Without, of course, lessening in any way the depth of emotion between them. If anything, it has underlined this feeling.

Avoid if you can, letting your heroine moan and your hero groan. A literary agent friend once told me she'd like five pounds for every moan that was ever written into a romantic novel! They always sound as if they're in so much pain.

Be original! What's happening on the printed page is being repeated in real life the world over, but if readers merely wanted to know the mechanics of sex, they'd read a textbook.

Readers do want to be enchanted by this wonderful love that's finally dawning between two characters they've come to know and identify with.

And they do know them by now, which is why you don't throw in a love scene on page two of your book, when each hardly knows the other's name.

Yes, it has been done like that, and the experts may get away with it. But I would never advise a beginner to write a love scene too early in the novel. Sexual tension must exist between the two, but it can be powerfully shown before the two of them ever reach the bedroom. *If they reach it.*

'Be original! What's happening on the printed page is being repeated in real life the world over, but if readers merely wanted to know the mechanics of sex, they'd read a text-book.'

Inside or outside the bedroom door?

Romantic novels no longer have to end outside the bedroom door. Indeed, the more gentle type of romance is undoubtedly less popular than it used to be. If, however, you are one of those authors who prefer to keep their romances chaste rather than sizzling, then seek out the publishers who cater for that style. The romance shelves of every public library are ready and waiting for the market study as well as for reading pleasure.

Writing love scenes means first of all losing your own inhibitions. Be prepared to put words into your characters' mouths that you wouldn't necessarily say yourself. Be prepared to let your characters make love in unlikely places if the story warrants it.

Above all, let your love scenes happen so naturally within the story that no other scene could possibly occur at that moment. And let them enjoy it! 'Making love' in this context doesn't only mean the physical sex act. Each scene that involves the extra charge of sexual attraction when hero and heroine are alone together is a love scene.

Always remember that the hero is falling in love too. Sometimes new authors forget this, but his emotions are every bit as important as the heroine's. He can be confused, angry, or even refuse to believe that this can be happening to him, but his masculine reactions will be different from her feminine ones. Show them differently.

There are right and wrong ways of writing love scenes. The description must be lyrical rather than clinical, but don't make them ridiculous by throwing in every romantic cliché you ever heard.

Ideally, at this point the heroine should be so overwhelmed by the man and by the emotion she feels for him that the thought of sin never enters her head. We're not trying to write soft porn. However, the period when your characters are making love in the novel - the moments leading up to it and the relaxation afterwards - is the perfect time for all the senses to be aroused.

To a reader totally involved in a romance, nothing can be more irritating than contrived interruptions. We've all read them. Some of us have written them. It used to be commonplace that the telephone would ring as the first kiss was about to happen. Just as the scene warmed up, there would be a knock on the door of the flat; if the lovers had actually reached the bedroom, a car's headlights would split the darkness and a returning housekeeper/flatmate/friend/brother would spoil the magic moment; the heroine herself would twist away in a sudden revelation of self-disgust at what she was doing, allowing this man who was a bit of a rake, to charm her - and what's more, she had been about to enjoy it!

'Writing love scenes means first of all losing your own inhibitions. Be prepared to put words into your characters' mouths that you wouldn't necessarily say yourself.'

Nowadays, as an independent, self-assured young woman she'd probably just go ahead and enjoy it. I'm not suggesting that all our readers are more permissive than they used to be, but undoubtedly there is a more open attitude to something that has been around for a very long time.

That's not to say that the romance has gone out of romantic novels, but we still have to be realistic, and reflect modern life. For a young heroine to throw up her hands in horror at a handsome man who makes it plain that he fancies her is as outdated as making every nice-girl heroine a bitch-lady's companion.

But how far does realism go? In real life, not every girl wants to be married. In fiction they almost always do by the end of the novel. By definition, romantic novels have happy endings, and hero and heroine *always* end up metaphorically going into the sunset together, and *usually* marriage is promised or intended; it is always the end result in a historical novel.

In a contemporary one too, even if the actual proposal is never written into the story, it's assumed or implied that a wedding will follow even the steamiest final scene. What's more important is that hero and heroine have a 'commitment' towards each other.

One essential point is that a heroine in a romantic novel is never promiscuous. She may be engaged to someone else when the novel begins, but is already discontented with her fiancé, and knows in her heart that she has made a mistake. She must let him down gently, and with good reason, to prevent the reader from thinking she's heartless.

She may already be married but separated from her husband, in which case, it will always be the estranged husband who comes back into her life to pick up where they left off, problems and all. And they will end up happily together.

In contemporary romance, a heroine may be divorced, as long as she wasn't the guilty partner, and is still getting over the trauma of it all. (This situation can provide a great depth of characterisation.) She could also be widowed.

In all of these cases, be extra careful if your story necessarily includes children, who complicate a plot considerably. If you can think up a plausible romance that includes children, then fine. But never let them and their problems take over the core of the novel, which is the love story between hero and heroine.

A hero can have been married before, and any of the previously mentioned situations also apply to him. It's sometimes unrealistic to read about so many charismatic heroes in their thirties who are still unmarried, or even uninterested in women. We know they exist, but not every romantic novel should have one!

Never describe any previous romantic relationship between the hero or heroine and some other person. The reader is only interested in the here-and-now and any extraneous love scenes will jar on her.

A past lover may try to come back into the heroine's life, but once she's met the hero, no one else can ever interest her, and a past lover is never so indiscreet as to mention the facts to anyone!

The Other Woman may try to poison the heroine's mind against the hero by intimating that they were once more than friends, but it will be made perfectly clear in due course that this is untrue.

Don't let this make you believe that every romantic novel is squeaky clean - that's not so! But there are certain accepted areas and some that are not so popular. Love scenes in both contemporary and historical novels should be written as passionately as the characters dictate. But tenderness and respect both play a part too. And above all, always, that sense of wonder that exists between two people on the brink of something very special in their lives.

The following is an example of a badly written love scene in a contemporary romance, followed by the same scene written more acceptably.

Version 1 – the wrong way

Janet was ready hours too early. She sat by the window of her hotel room, hoping she looked all right. Her heart fluttered every time she thought of his strong masculine arms and that powerful bronzed leashed strength of his, remembering the way his voice had rasped thickly at her as he'd asked her to go dancing with him that evening.

Was she going to be held in those powerful, muscular, hair-roughened arms at last? Would she feel his firm sensual lips plundering hers? The thought of it was enough to make her feel quivery through every fibre of her being. Tonight was the night.

When he rapped impatiently on her door, her feet became lead weights. She could hardly drag them to the door to open it. How was she ever going to dance all night? Or perhaps dancing wasn't the only thing on Luke's wicked mind, she thought lecherously, her eyes beginning to gleam.

'Ready?' Luke's hot eyes raked her body in the new dress she had bought specially. 'You look good. How did you know I liked blue?'

'I didn't. Shall we go?'

The evening was nice, but she couldn't wait for Luke to take her back to the hotel room. She kept looking at the clock. As they danced, he bent her backwards, arching her willing body, kissing her lips. He didn't care who saw them. Neither did she. His kiss was hard, pulsing, bruising. She tasted blood. She tingled all over.

At last they got back to the hotel room.

'I've been waiting for this,' he said thickly.

'So have I. Oh, Luke!' she moaned.

'Don't talk,' he commanded. He lifted her in his arms, the powerful muscles rippling beneath his jacket, and carried her towards the bedroom . . .

Good grief! (to use yet another cliché . . .) That scene is crammed with mistakes. The dialogue is trite. It's riddled with clichés. There's a lot of repetition. Despite an attempt to make it racy, it's a cold scene, lacking emotion, and with sleazy undertones for what's meant to be a gentle love scene. The heroine should never talk (or think) lecherously. She's moaning, probably because her back's being broken in two. The writing is clumsy, and the girl seems shop-soiled. There's no feeling of magic between them. Incidentally, her feet can't actually become lead weights. Luke could hardly heave her around the dancefloor, let alone fancy her.

Version 2 – the right way

Janet was ready ages before Luke arrived. By then, she was so tense she wondered how to deal with it. She knew that her feelings towards him had changed. If she were honest, she had stopped hating him a long while ago, and she could no longer deny the sexual attraction between them. But she had no wish to be added to his list of affairs.

She shivered, looking at her own reflection in the mirror, knowing she had worn the new silvery blue dress because blue was his favourite colour. Perhaps she was being a fool after all. She should have made some excuse not to go with him - but she had no intention of letting him think she was nervous of being alone with him . . .

Janet heard him knock at her door and felt her heart leap. When she let him in, he studied her slowly from head to toe, and she felt the warmth in her cheeks as she read the approval in his eyes. All that, and something more . . .

Dancing in his arms was like floating on a cloud. His lips touched her cheek as they danced, and she knew how easy, how very easy it would be to fall in love with him. Or had she done that a long time ago, so gradually that she hadn't realised it was happening?

'In one way I never want this night to end,' Luke whispered against her hair. 'And yet I wish it could go on forever. I don't want to say goodnight and let you go like Cinderella. I'm so afraid you'll have vanished by morning.'

'Are you?' Janet said weakly, her voice dry in her throat, because he had never seemed capable of such tenderness before. 'You know I'll still be here, Luke. I'm your promotions girl -'

Luke's hold on her tightened. As they slowly circled the dance floor, she could feel the pressure of his fingers against her spine. His voice was suddenly deeper, his mouth no more than a warm breath from hers in the crush of people.

'Don't you know that I want you to be *my* girl?' His voice deepened, its tone more urgent. 'Let's get out of here and go back to the hotel, darling. I can't say all that I want to with all these people around.'

She looked up at him, and the flippant words she intended to say disappeared as she recognised the desire in his eyes. It matched some primitive emotion in herself at that moment, and she nodded wordlessly. The time for fencing was over, and all that had gone before had been leading up to this magical awareness of mind and body that she knew instinctively was love.

Summing Up

- Forget your own inhibitions when writing your love scenes.

- Don't write breathless prose that invites ridicule from readers.

- Steamy can still be tender and romantic, or as erotic as the novel dictates.

- Be aware of the nature of the characters you have created. You created them after all, so don't let them down.

Chapter Eight
Values – Old and New

Yes, they still apply. However trendy or sensual or blatantly sexy the novel, there are still old-fashioned values for authors to uphold, and still certain 'rules' about what is and is not acceptable, both to editors and readers.

Most readers infinitely prefer a one-man, one-woman relationship in a contemporary or historical romance. Above all, they want the heroine to get her man, and for the couple to transcend all the difficulties the author has put in their way.

Chivalrous, gallant, polite, tender . . . such qualities in a hero's character are not to be despised, even though some of those actual words may be updated. It's the way that an author uses those qualities in her novel that will make a character cosily old-fashioned or very desirable and irresistible. We may not use all those exact words nowadays, but the meaning will still be there.

Sexual equality may be a fact of life, but there are still millions of women who prefer a man to open a door for her, to bring her flowers, to take her out for dinner and pay for it, and to see that she gets safely home afterwards.

At one time, as in the heyday of Hollywood films, every hero, and possibly the heroine too, would be smoking a cigarette, in that strangely intimate world of two people enclosed in their own smoky cloud. The Other Woman often blew a stream of smoke into the air to demonstrate how sophisticated she was.

Such ploys are as outmoded as they sound. Heroes may still smoke an expensive cigar or cheroot, but since the anti-smoking campaign and health warnings generally, we've all become aware of the lingering smell of smoke in the hair and clothes and on the breath, not to mention the yellow-stained fingers! Not the most attractive thoughts when applied to a romantic heroine, who is rarely caught smoking in today's novels, and never in historicals.

'Yes, they still apply. However trendy or sensual or blatantly sexy the novel, there are still old-fashioned values for authors to uphold.'

There are far better ways to demonstrate that someone is slick or sophisticated or bitchy than by letting them smoke cigarettes. Good characterisation should do that for you, especially your dialogue.

Generally, anything that is taken to be anti-social should be avoided, especially with regard to the hero and heroine. Obviously, you will allow other characters to have different standards, to provide the foil for the hero's sterling qualities, for instance!

Erotica

'There's nothing new about writing erotic fiction. The difference nowadays is that it's no longer hidden between brown paper covers, or on under-the-counter book shelves.'

As was said in chapter 2, however, we can't ignore the emergence of the erotica specifically intended for women readers. These books will be heavily overloaded with sex scenes, and the publishers state frankly that the books are intended to titillate. The purpose of them, as in every other kind of novel, is to entertain in a particular way.

There's nothing new about writing erotic fiction. The difference nowadays is that it's no longer hidden between brown paper covers, or on under-the-counter book shelves. It's blatantly available in airports, reputable bookshops and in libraries. It's a market in which you may well be interested.

Some of the most prestigious publishers are now including erotic fiction in their lists. Again, whether or not you consider this to be romance is subjective. Certainly you will need to go much further with your characters and to invent wilder and frequently shocking storylines. This is undoubtedly why most of the authors of the published novels use exotic pseudonyms.

There's little censorship in today's novels, either in language or content, so if you feel that this may be your forte, read some of the books to see if they suit your reading and writing tastes. Send for the tip-sheets from the publishers and make up your mind. Some of the tip-sheets alone may shock you. But then again, they may not. This may be just what you've been waiting for.

You may consider that erotica is no more than an extension of the old-style bodice-rippers. Just be prepared to write about some pretty traumatic happenings to your heroine. Rape may certainly be one of them, and will be described in as much graphic detail as you care to write.

Differences between erotica and traditional romances

It is graphic detail that marks one of the main differences between erotica and contemporary romances of the more traditional kind, where rape will never be described in any great detail. It rarely occurs in the latter kind of novel. If it does, it will have happened in the past, and will inevitably have coloured the heroine's attitude to life and love. In this way, the fact that it happened at all can be used as a useful catalyst to the direction the heroine's life will take from then on.

Rape will be a shameful thing in the heroine's past, despite her innocence. Whatever references to it there are in the story, the explanations will make it quite clear how abhorrent the whole episode was. By the time the hero discovers why she's constantly rejecting him, the reader will be in complete sympathy with her reasons for a deep mistrust of men, and feel warmed towards the caring hero for gradually restoring her trust, and teaching her how to love again.

A rape scene is not a love scene. In a strong, steamy historical novel, rapes do occur if the story calls for such action. They should never happen so frequently that one wonders how the poor girl survives.

If you're not afraid to tackle such scenes, which can be dramatic and violent, sometimes ugly, sometimes very poignant, then almost anything goes - providing you've staged the right setting for your characters, their situations, and the stormy conflicts in the novel.

The key point is never to include a rape scene unless it's there for a specific fictional purpose, to move the plot along in some way and to allow the characters' lives to change direction. However explicit such a scene, write it with integrity.

Many of the characteristics, listed below do not fit into traditional romances but would certainly fit into erotica, and many into mainstream romantic fiction as well.

Drug-taking should be avoided in a romance. So should alcoholism, unless it happened in a character's past to someone close to him, which coloured his views on drinking.

Gambling can sometimes be a hero's failing that can be put to his advantage, but more generally in a historical novel than a contemporary. My hero in *Killigrew Clay* (Rowena Summers) made good use of a dormant gambling talent to help save the family fortunes, thus turning a 'failing' into a virtue.

Such 'flaws' as a primitive need for speed and excitement finding an outlet in the world of motor-racing, or a lust for danger expressed in hang-gliding or mountaineering or deep-sea diving are acceptable in the hero, even the heroine, as long as she doesn't lose her femininity by pursuing what were once considered male activities. But what must never be in any doubt is the heterosexuality of the hero and heroine.

In contemporary romances, fringe groups such as racial fanatics, religious sects, or secret societies are out. So are incest, homosexuality, murder. Mass riots, mass violence, or muggings do not fit into contemporary romances.

Strangely, an occasional kidnapping may be acceptable. A hero may kidnap his child in order to bring the heroine back into his life, with never any risk or hurt or danger to their child. The heroine may be 'kidnapped' by the hero, for reasons of his own, that will inevitably end in a love scene and not violence.

Heroes and villains

The old style of passive heroine who does nothing in the novel except weep or look beautiful, and is no more than an accessory to the hero, is out of date. Today's heroine must be self-confident, independent, capable of thinking for herself, but still indisputably feminine. Strident women don't make romantic heroines.

Fictional heroes are generally tall, without necessarily being dark and handsome anymore, though they're rarely described as pale-skinned or blond. Dark heroes are still the most popular, but will be rugged in appearance rather than too perfectly featured. The athletic outdoors man is always attractive to readers, and so is the powerful business tycoon.

But the once-popular overbearing arrogance is dreary and too predictable, and what modern girl would put up with such a man? Who can take seriously the kind of old-style romance where the heroine hankers after a man who is boringly hateful until the very end of the book? Most women would have told him to get lost long before the final page!

It's a peculiar fact that readers will accept more of a rakish character in a historical hero than in a contemporary one. The language he uses can be stronger, more blasphemous - as long as it fits into the mood of the particular scene - and the writing can be altogether more lusty in every sense. Perhaps it's because we're more distant from historical times, and the world of a historical romance doesn't seem uncomfortably near to things that might be recognisable in our own lives, or things that we read in the newspapers every day. Whatever the reason, all the 'rules' I have mentioned in this chapter have been successfully broken in historical romances with exclusively imaginary characters. How you deal with real people in a historical romance is another matter altogether, and one that needs special care.

Historical romances

There are various kinds of historical romantic novels. Those that are light and totally fictional, sometimes called 'fancy-dress historicals', will probably contain no reference to real people at all. As with a contemporary romance the background may be an invented island or town, and all the characters will have come from your own imagination. Apart from research for your chosen era, you have no problems.

When you write a novel with an authentic background, you have many more. Almost all my historical romances are set in real places, where my characters encounter real people, and many have battle scenes or factual confrontations. How to find out about such things will be dealt with in the chapter on research.

An author must be very careful not to put a real character into a place he couldn't possibly have been on that precise date. Nor should she put words into his mouth that are the exact opposite to that person's recorded views.

You can't, metaphorically speaking, pick up the American Civil War and transpose it into a War of the Roses setting. If all the history books refer to a royal person as being short and fat, you can't describe him as being tall and willowy because you think it makes him sound more attractive (although people do!)

There are ways to gloss over tricky moments in a romantic novel as in any other. There are ways of avoiding saying something you're not sure about. But if you *do* say it, be sure it's accurate. If it's not, the editor will almost certainly spot it. If she doesn't, and the book is published, you can be sure plenty of knowledgeable readers will spot a mistake. Letters of complaint will arrive at the publishers, and they will be less enthusiastic about your next novel. Even worse, readers may not want to read more of your books.

Readers can be very faithful to the authors they like, and will buy their books avidly. But that does not mean they will not turn away if they feel an author has let them down, perhaps by letting careless writing and mistakes slip through, or by allowing a fall in general standards.

Authors provide entertainment, and also a service. A reader who has paid out good money for a novel wants to feel that this is an author who cares about her work, and about what she is saying.

A bored author will result in a bored reader, while one who puts all the enthusiasm she knows into her craft will make the pages sparkle and the characters come to life. It may still not be the best book in the world, but, in my opinion, that enthusiasm is as vital as talent.

It takes more than talent to write novels. It takes determination and self-discipline, a belief in yourself without being egotistical - the first rejection letter will soon dispel that - and it also takes love. Love for your characters and care over what happens to them.

Characters are people, and people are all different and yet in many ways all the same. By that, I mean that we are all capable of the same emotions, hopes, fears, dreams. It's the individual mixture of these traits that makes each of us unique. And it's that mix of qualities that we try to give to each of our fictional friends. Each one must be as unique as the real thing. No robots allowed!

'You can't, metaphorically speaking, pick up the American Civil War and transpose it into a War of the Roses setting.'

Long after I've finished writing a novel, the story still stays with me, still part of me. I'm reluctant to let go of these people I've come to know better than my own family because I know all their faults and failures as well as their triumphs.

The adrenaline flows when an author begins to write a novel. There's a feeling of anticipation, of starting out on a great adventure with the characters, and if you're sufficiently involved with your story, that excitement is carried through to the end of the book.

When I'm writing my books, I like to think I've kept faith with my characters, and if that's an old-fashioned view, then I don't think it's such a bad one.

Summing Up

- There are still some taboos. Check them out.
- Keep your characters consistent to what you first decided for them.
- Write your novel for the readership you are aiming for.
- Read some erotic fiction before attempting it.
- If it makes you uneasy, try writing something else.

Chapter Nine
Research

You've just thought up a marvellous idea for a romantic novel. Your hero will be a pavement artist who is really the son of a rich French nobleman; your country-born heroine has just become a London taxi-driver. Intriguing for any reader.

You won't bother with all that stuff about planning and plotting. You know where to begin. You'll get them talking right away, when they meet on an evening cruise on the River Thames.

You rush right in, hot onto the keyboard, filled with supreme confidence. The dialogue will be a mass of interesting little details to intrigue the readers, all about his French chateau background and how he came to be painting on the London pavement, and her experiences in learning her new job and getting her licence . . . full of fascinating detail . . .

At this point you come to a complete stop before you've covered more than a couple of pages, if you've even got that far. You realise you don't know these characters. Their lives are a total blank - you know absolutely nothing about their imaginary selves, and the lifestyles you've decided for them. Your book will be just as empty, if you don't find out the relevant facts about them before you begin.

Research means no more than that. Yet the thought of it can throw beginners into as big a panic as the idea of writing a synopsis. While you may be the kind of author who can get by without writing a detailed synopsis, some research is always necessary, and it needn't be as traumatic as many people imagine. Many authors, myself included, consider that research is one of the most enjoyable parts of writing a novel, especially a historical one.

You can sometimes get carried away by the books you're reading in the name of research and spend more time than you intended on it. It's never wasted. Even if you're not using much of the information you're absorbing, the feeling of the time, characters, background, etc, will make your writing come alive with confidence.

But supposing you're writing a contemporary romance set in your own town, where you know every street and cinema, and the time of the novel is the present? There'll be no problems with outdated fashion and hairstyles and slang, and all the difficult things you need to know for historical novels that you craftily intend to avoid.

So now why bother with research? You're writing about what you know, which is meant to be the easiest way for beginners. You don't need to do any research. It will be a waste of time.

Well, unless you have a superhuman memory, your knowledge of quite familiar things will probably play tricks with you. If you set a love scene in a local park at sunset, you may not quite capture that scent of roses with the evening dew on them, mingled with whatever other flora the park displays. It will be a subtle, elusive scent, particular to that one place, and you probably won't describe it perfectly unless you go there, breathe it all in, record it immediately.

If your background is that close to home, always go there and absorb the atmosphere for yourself. Don't rely on memory alone. A fresh, instant impression will make the description all the more vivid in your book.

Is that too difficult? Or does it all sound too easy? Research can be as simple or as complicated as you care to make it. Still considering a local background for your novel? Try giving snap answers to the following questions.

Check your facts

- What does the facade of your local town hall look like, and what colour is the stonework?

- Does your railway station have tubs or displays of flowers on the platforms?

- Is there a comprehensive school near you?

- How many libraries in your town?

- Is your town twinned with a European one, and what is its name?

- If you live in a coastal holiday town, what entertainments are there on the pier?

- What colour carpets and curtains does the newest nightspot in town have?

Maybe none of these things would occur in your novel. But I doubt if you can recall half of them accurately, even if you frequent some of the places every day. Well, probably not the nightspot, not every day.

If you wanted to write about any one of those ordinary places in your own town, you would need to go there and do a bit of checking, to make sure your facts are true. If you were wrong, all your neighbours would complain that you don't know what you're talking about when, naturally, they all buy your book!

That's research. And that's the easiest kind. If it's that easy, why not make your book as accurate as you can?

Research for contemporary novels is easier than for historicals, merely because everything we need to know is all around us, still breathing, and ready for the taking - or asking. You can find out about unusual occupations by writing to an appropriate organisation and requesting information, stating that you want it for your novel, if only out of politeness.

It may be that you won't get any reply since you're not a genuine job applicant, but usually people are only too pleased to help.

Of course, you'll eavesdrop. All authors do, consciously or subconsciously. You hear some marvellously revealing conversations in bus queues or in pubs. You won't record them word for word in your head or in a notebook, unless you want to risk being cited for slander, but you'll absorb the essence of dialogue between certain types of people.

Listening in

You may well get an idea for additional characters for your novel by 'listening in'. This is research too. Even if you base a character on a real one, people rarely recognise themselves, but it's as well to invent them rather than risk it.

People are always willing to talk about themselves, their lives and their jobs. If you can get into conversation with a ballet dancer, pop singer, croupier, farmer, horse-breeder, fairground wheeler-dealer or whoever, you can learn all sorts of interesting personal snippets that may never be apparent from a source such as an information fact sheet.

Treat older folk with respect, and although they'll probably view you with a little suspicion at first, their memories will usually be vividly given. Remember though, that their facts may be somewhat distorted with time and it pays to back up their ramblings, no matter how colourful and fascinating, with a visit to your local reference library.

I spent hours driving around the Somerset Levels when I was researching for my historical novel *Willow Harvest* (Rowena Summers). The area is renowned for its willow-growing and basket-making, both of which play a major part in my novel. The old methods have changed little, and it was still possible to see the willows (called withies in Somerset) growing and drying as they used to, and to see some of the basket-makers at work, and to absorb the rich flavour of the scene at first hand.

All this was supplemented by reading as many books on the subject as I could get, and by the added reminiscences of a friend whose father had been a basket-maker. How grateful I was to have such a friend! When you start to ask around, it's often amazing how much information you can find close at hand.

'Many contemporary romances are set in foreign and exotic backgrounds. Do you think all the authors have been there? Of course not.'

Foreign and exotic backgrounds

Many contemporary romances are set in foreign and exotic backgrounds. Do you think all the authors have been there? Of course not. Especially when each novel they write is set in a more glamorous setting than the last! They'd have to spend all their time travelling instead of writing. But from their novels, you would think they knew each place intimately, and that's because they researched each location thoroughly.

In your home town it was easy . . . and some authors will say you can't get the complete flavour of any background without going there. But obviously that's not always possible. You must still, however, make it seem so authentic that the reader is instantly transported to that tropical island or sun-baked Spanish beach or sophisticated French casino.

While I'm writing a novel - which is almost all the time, since I'm a compulsive writer - my desk is in total chaos, with books and brochures and bits of paper everywhere.

I use maps to locate the area where I'll set my romance, and am especially careful over distances my characters have to travel. A horse can't travel as far as a train in one day without dropping dead from exhaustion.

A sprinkling of real towns and imaginary locations makes a good mix.

Names of real streets can be used, providing you don't put a bazaar into a residential area, or a hospital into the ocean! I describe interiors and exhibits of such places as museums with accuracy, since details of these can easily be found in any appropriate reference book.

When I go on holiday, I come home loaded down with booklets of any interesting and possibly useful places I've seen, and I take research photos as well as the usual holiday snaps. This is painless research, and incidentally, all of these things can be claimed against income tax.

Guide books give information about travel and details of food and drink relevant to the country. Old films on television can be helpful, as long as the settings haven't been over-glamorised. Phrase books provide the occasional foreign sentence, but don't overdo it. And be quite sure of what your characters are saying!

Travel brochures are a great source of information: not only do they describe actual places but they often include little bits of folklore as part of the tourist attractions. Travel brochures can sketch in a background you can then research further at your local library. But always beware of making your book begin to sound more like a travelogue than a romantic novel.

Every author should get to know her librarians. Mine are enormously helpful. They take a personal interest in the books I request, and in the pile I take home for each new novel, asking if this is what the next one will be about.

They have got used to my requests for books on subjects such as witchcraft, pot-holing, the Indian Mutiny, flower-arranging, tea-planting in Ceylon, Eastern jewellery, Scottish clans, cider-making and the Somerset apple orchards. Now, of course, the Internet search engines have helped enormously regarding research.

I constantly add to my own reference books. I have books on costume and fashion through the ages, an excellent dictionary of historical slang, marriage customs and folklore, crafts, different cultures, biographies of notable people, books about different countries, ancient occupations, anything and everything that I think could be of future use. (See Appendix 2.) They can be claimed against income tax.

Details can be found from unlikely sources, and much closer to home. In *Love's Sweet Music* (Jean Saunders), my hero was a concert pianist, and I made him more human by letting him relate something about the background of each piece of music before he played it. I got most of the information from the record sleeves in my own collection of classical records.

Historical research can take a good deal of time. If you're describing in detail a battle such as Culloden, as I did in my novel *Scarlet Rebel* (Jean Saunders), you need to know not only the battle strategy, but the visual appearance of the uniforms on both sides (in this case only one side wore uniforms), the names and characters of the real officers involved, the time of day the battle commenced and ended, the weather on that particular day.

Without attention to such details, your work will look careless and it won't have that true ring of credibility. You can't invent an officer for a recorded historical battle if it can be easily proven in a dozen reference books that such an officer could never have existed! There's an added bonus in getting facts right that may not be apparent to you. It gives the author a subtle confidence in the writing that shows through.

In researching for a historical novel, where the time element often dictates what actual events you're going to cover, you must sift out the important facts and discard those that won't have any bearing on your plot.

When you need to give a large amount of information in your book, always try to filter it in through dialogue between the characters, so that they are telling the facts. This isn't always practical, but if the page runs the risk of being overloaded with details, then try to bring your characters into the prose. Involve them.

If you are writing a dramatic court scene, for instance, describe it all, but describe it through your characters' emotional response to what they're seeing, rather than using straight narrative description. The scene becomes alive, instead of being static.

I'll give away one of my secrets. When I'm researching for a new novel, especially a historical romance, I invariably begin in the children's library. The research for *Scarlet Rebel* began with a Ladybird book called *Bonnie Prince Charlie.*

There are several reasons for this. One is the practical one that you simply can't wade through every book published on a given subject. By going first to the children's library, you'll find the facts more clearly written than anywhere else. You'll have illustrations that bring historical scenes vividly to life for young eyes, and a clear outline of any chronological data. Such a book can often decide for you whether your subject has enough 'meat' in it for you to weave a romance around it.

I consult as many as I can find, and then move on to the adult sections and reference sections. But those marvellous children's books have given me many a clear first insight into a background I might otherwise have left alone.

However you do your research, it's as important to your novel as the actual writing. Whether it's as simple as knowing if Sorrento has a sandy beach, or when crinolines went out of fashion, or the names of generals in battle, get your facts right. Skimping on your research could mean the difference between rejection and publication.

For more detailed advice on research, see *How to Research Your Novel* by Jean Saunders, in the Allison & Busby Writers' Guides series.

'When you need to give a large amount of information in your book, always try to filter it in through dialogue between the characters, so that they are telling the facts.'

Summing Up

- Don't skimp on research.
- Create the right atmosphere for your readers.
- Ask the man who knows.
- Enjoy getting it right.

Chapter Ten
Getting It All Together

Visual thinking is every author's magic wand, and the ability to turn your dream pictures into words that are as instantly vivid to your reader is magical indeed. Your own style, the author's voice that is uniquely yours, is what develops and grows as you gain experience and confidence in your writing. Human quirks being what they are, most people are extremely reticent about telling friends and family when they begin to write. They hide manuscripts in their cupboards, as if they were something shameful. Some will only write when everyone is out of the house, and then send a manuscript off secretly.

It's only on that wonderful day when an editor actually offers to pay money for their article, poem, short story or novel, that they confess all. Until then, they have been closet authors!

But now, suddenly and gloriously, it's not just scribbling that they do. It's serious work. They can hold their heads high, freed from the odd little 'stigma' that any creative work makes people a bit 'different'.

Perhaps none of that applies to you, but it applies to many people that I've met. When we're unsuccessful, even if we strive for years, 'the writing' can be suspect. When it sells we're seen in a different light. Everyone loves a winner! But how do we write the kind of romantic novel that elevates us from kitchen scribe to published author?

The ingredients that go into the making of a novel can be as complex and yet as basic as in any cake mixture. Using the same analogy, it's the way we put them all together that makes it a success or failure.

By now, you know many of the ingredients: good characterisation, a believable plot, a story that moves and isn't static, dialogue that makes fictional characters sound like real people, detailed research so that even if we've never been to the setting we've described, we convey the feel of the place.

'Visual thinking is every author's magic wand, and the ability to turn your dream pictures into words that are as instantly vivid to your reader is magical indeed.'

But ingredients alone don't make a novel. Imagine a beautiful three-tiered wedding cake, perfectly proportioned and capable of standing alone on its base, no matter how fragile it seems. Without a solid foundation and a construction that stops it from toppling sideways and crumbling into a soggy mass, that cake would be uneatable.

So with a novel. A solid foundation to support all the other ingredients, and a construction that gives it shape and substance and form, are essential.

The theme is your foundation. The plot is your construction. If you've got the ingredients right, the end result should be a perfect, beautifully rounded piece of work, balanced throughout.

Don't spoil it by throwing in an extra handful of currants - minor characters who have fascinating stories of their own to tell, but nothing at all to do with the main story.

Overdo the amounts of butter or eggs, and you'll make the cake too mushy - too much sentimentality will make your reader cringe with embarrassment. Similarly with too much sugar . . .

Too much flour will clog the cake and make it heavy - include a fine mixture of research detail to whet the reader's appetite, but never so much that it weighs the book down and disguises its real flavour.

'But all romance readers have something in common. They read romantic novels for pleasure, relaxation and entertainment.'

Romance readers

Enough of all this. Let's get down to details. Put yourself in the role of Miss Average Romance Reader for a moment, if she exists at all. Since readers come in all age groups and from all spheres of society, she is as hard to define as a member of an extinct race.

But all romance readers have something in common. They read romantic novels for pleasure, relaxation and entertainment. Imagine that you, as a reader are going into a bookshop to buy a novel to read on holiday, or during coffee breaks at the office, or with your feet up after the children have gone to bed.

Look at the mass of novels on the romance shelves. What do you see first? The cover illustration, obviously. And this is one area which the author has no control. If she's lucky, it will portray her story in exactly the way she imagined it. It doesn't always, and the author just hopes that the publishers will do better for her next time!

Also on the cover are the title and the author's name. Readers don't bother too much about an author's name unless it's been recommended by a friend or hyped - that is, promoted - in the media, or unless they have read something by that author before and liked it well enough to recognise the name.

The title is the label which draws many a reader to a book she might otherwise overlook. Make your title memorable. Never underestimate the impact it can have on a browsing shopper. Who can forget such emotive titles as *Jamaica Inn, Gone with the Wind, Stay with Me Till Morning, Catcher in the Rye, Brief Encounter, The Forsyte Saga, The Thorn Birds*? Each conjures up a picture, obvious or curious, but each one stays in the memory. Weak titles often indicate a weak book. Let yours say something about your story as concisely and vividly as possible.

Next, Miss Average Romance Reader will probably turn the book to read the blurb on the back. This will usually have been written by the publisher, but sometimes the author is asked to write it. If so, don't be shy about your book.

This is no time to slink back into the closet, blushing with false modesty. It's your first opportunity to tell the world that here is a rousing/lusty/sensitive/ tender romance (not all at once!), with a fast-paced story and fiery/spirited/ dashing characters. Reveal some, but not all, of the novel's content - just enough to intrigue and entice, and make Miss Average Romance Reader open the book and scan the first page.

First page . . . remember? She'll glance down it. Her mind will register how long or short the blocks of prose are, which may colour her reactions; she may see a sprinkling of dialogue; an early hint as to what the story is all about, any specific location or climatic details; the names of the characters, which she'll want to know as soon as possible.

Being an experienced romance reader, she'll know by now whether she wants to turn the page. If she does, and the early promise of page one continues, she'll do one of two things. She'll turn to the end of chapter one, to see if it intrigues her enough to glance at the beginning of chapter two. Or else she'll have a quick look at the last page. Quick enough to see if it's a satisfyingly happy ending, not long enough to spoil the book for her if she decides to buy it. And she hasn't decided yet.

Miss Average Romance Reader will then start to flip through the pages. She'll be looking for those love scenes, and when she finds one, she'll probably stand and read it. Personal taste decides again. If it passes, she'll flip through some more, and consider the mixture of dialogue and description and action throughout the book.

Finally, if she thinks it looks as if it's worth the money, which she may or may not have checked already, then she'll buy it. And if you think all this is imaginary, I promise you I've done my own check on Miss Average Romance Reader, lurking behind the paperback shelves in many a bookshop or newsagent's.

So what comes out of all this market research? Readers look primarily for a book that they expect to keep them interested from beginning to end. What every one of them wants to read, and what every author should seek to write, is a page-turner. Colourful and exciting when the story calls for it; tender and emotional when characterisation demands it.

For an author to sustain that page-turning quality, there must always be an element of suspense in any romance. Not necessarily in the thriller sense of the word, but in not making your story so predictable that the reader knows the end halfway through the book.

By then she will know the identity of the hero in a contemporary romance, though not necessarily in a historical. That still shouldn't prevent the twists and turns of the plot creating believable incidents and keeping up the sparkling tone and the smooth pace of the novel.

Suspense can be usefully created, for instance, if there's a time limit within your book; if the characters have to complete some task by a certain time, when all seems against it.

If you can think in scenes, try to make each scene lead on from the one before it. Read published novels to see how effortlessly, or sometimes startlingly, other authors achieve this. Whatever the effect, it was almost certainly designed to happen that way.

Note especially what happens at the end of each chapter. This is where the author tempts the reader to go on to the next chapter every night, rounding off the day with their fictional quota of nostalgia or pulsing passion.

The author's aim is to make that baited hook at the end of the chapter so enticing that the reader just can't resist taking a peep at the next chapter and before she knows it, she's reading on . . . and on . . .

How do you achieve this? You can give a blatant hint of what's about to happen next or be more subtle, driving the reader mad with curiosity: the chapter can end on a knife-edge of tension - perhaps a revelation between the characters, or a statement that temporarily destroys their illusions about each other. Alternatively, end it gently, like the calm before the storm - the reader will begin to suspect that things can't go on like this for much longer. Write it in such a way that she can't possibly wait until tomorrow to see what happens. She will be compelled to turn the pages now, and to blazes with having to get up early in the morning!

Happy endings or almost

A romantic novel builds steadily in excitement and tension as the story unfolds, until the last and most important scene, where the hero and heroine finally reach their happy ending, and the reader is left with a feeling of pleasure that after all everything has turned out well.

Don't make this scene too short. Allow the reader to enjoy to the full the final pages of vicarious romance that she's been sharing with the characters. She'll feel cheated if you tie up the ends too neatly and swiftly.

Beginners often fail to realise this. They're so keen to type those two exciting words, 'The End', that they skimp on the most significant scene of all. Any explanations that need to be made, any misunderstandings still be to cleared up, *must* be clarified now, or else the reader will start asking what happened about so-and-so, and feel let down when there's no answer.

If the author has written 192 pages in a short romance, or anything up to 500 pages or even more in a long historical, to relate the story, then to wind up everything in a few short sentences should make her feel dissatisfied too.

A romantic novel will always end with a scene involving the two main characters, and rarely anyone else. Who wants anyone else at such intimate moments? And they are *always* intimate moments, whether they're written euphorically or chastely, with a sweet kiss and a promise of marriage, or in a sizzling and fiery embrace that leaves little to the imagination; the final scene in a romantic novel is nearly always a love scene.

Nearly always . . . In a family saga romance there is often a scene of more introspection on the part of the heroine, or sometimes the hero. A moment of nostalgia that is encapsulated in the reader's mind, and leads her on to give a sigh of satisfaction at the end of the last page.

How that scene is written will be dictated not only by the novel but, more importantly, by the characters themselves. If they are true to themselves, the ending will be written in the only way applicable to them. They'll be ending their story.

All the 'rules' of writing romantic novels have been broken at one time or another by an author who has one over-riding quality - the ability to tell a story. Who has not read a bestseller that defies all the so-called rules, and yet is so compelling that the reader cannot put it down?

We would all like to be that author, but for those who are still having difficulty in knowing where to begin, it's sensible to follow the basic requirement of the genre. Once your confidence has grown, then fly your own wings.

And *when* to begin? One of the marvellous things about writing is that it can be done anywhere, at any age, in short bursts or long stretches, if you're lucky enough to be able to devote all your time to it. I juggled my writing around my children's schooltimes and a part-time job at first. Many people work full-time and can only snatch an hour or so in the early morning or late evening, or on the train travelling to and from work.

What's more important is that you do begin to try to write something every day. If you can't manage that, then form your own writing habit. Your mind will gradually learn that this is 'writing time', and that perceptive mood will be upon you as easily as slipping into an old coat.

When you can't sit down and put pen to paper, let the 'writing' carry on in your head. I've thought up many a basic plot over the ironing. I've 'rehearsed' dialogue while walking to the shops. Those awful writers' blocks you hear about are less likely to descend on you if you train yourself in this way.

Yes, they happen to everyone at some stage or other. Some days the writing flows more easily than others. Some days you will think that you'll never write another word because everything that comes out of your head reads back like rubbish. After more than eighty published novels, there are still days when I close the door on my study and go off on a shopping spree, rather than be frustrated by a fruitless writing stint.

But I've learned to avoid blocks to some extent by never sitting down to a blank sheet of paper without knowing what my first sentences are going to be. I rehearse them in my head. Try it. It works.

And here's one last tip. Instead of finishing your work tidily for the day at the end of a chapter, use one more sheet of paper, and write the leading sentences of the next chapter. Then you've already got a head-start on tomorrow's thinking. You're cheating that block! And you'll be amazed how soon you'll be getting it all together.

'When you can't sit down and put pen to paper, let the 'writing' carry on in your head. I've thought up many a basic plot over the ironing. I've 'rehearsed' dialogue while walking to the shops.'

Summing Up

- Try to think in scenes.
- Forget about writer's block.
- Put the suspense into your romance.
- Happy - or hopeful endings.
- Make them laugh, make them cry... make them wait.

Chapter Eleven
Surviving Rejection

It's a horrible moment when any piece of creative work is rejected and comes back to its owner like a homing pigeon. All those weeks, months, even years of work, have been turned down by some faceless person, with perhaps no more than a polite printed slip of paper returning your wonderful romantic novel.

At best, you may get an encouraging letter, pointing out a few flaws in the writing, the content, etc, and intimating that the editor would be pleased to see your next novel - but it will still be a rejection.

No matter how much you snarl at the name at the bottom of the letter, or plead to anyone who will listen that you were in the midst of a family crisis when you wrote *this* one, and of course the next one will be better, it was *this* novel that had to stand the editorial test. And the only way to survive rejection is to pick yourself up and begin all over again.

If it's any comfort, some of our best-known authors suffered in exactly the same way before they became instantly recognised names. One popular romantic author had seven novels rejected before finally being accepted - and has gone on to become a very big name.

That's determination, the will to succeed - call it anything you care to, but if you have that urge, that need to write, then the thought of rejection will be one more incentive to make your romance one that the editors won't put aside and mark 'return to sender'.

And if you're 'fortunate' enough for an editor to put a few comments in your rejection letter, pause for a moment in your urge to scream that she doesn't know what she's talking about and can't recognise quality when she sees it.

Yes, she can. Yes, she does know what she's talking about. That's why she's a romance editor and you're an unpublished author. That's why she has the power and authority to turn you down and suggest that you try again.

'It's a horrible moment when any piece of creative work is rejected and comes back to its owner like a homing pigeon.'

Once you've got over the wish to strangle her, read her letter again. It may tell you that you've written a nice, competent novel, but the signs are telling you that it doesn't stand out among the many that are submitted.

The letter may say more between the lines than the kind words the editor has written. Yes they *are* kind. Editors are very busy people. They didn't ask for your manuscript, did they? If it's exactly what they want, they'll buy it. If not, be grateful for any help they give you. You're getting advice from the top, and if you're short-sighted enough not to heed it, then you deserve to go on getting manuscripts rejected.

The editor may suggest that you need to do more research, that there are many superfluous passages - padding - and obscure meanings. Characters may all be too similar, so that none of them stand out clearly. She may even hint that you seemed bored with your novel by the time you got halfway through it. Or that your grammar and punctuation weren't quite up to standard.

She may even say bluntly that the plot is too slight or the characters are wooden. (Next time an actor is on TV talking about the character he's playing, listen to him. He'll describe that fictional character as if he's as real to him as his own brother. That's how your characters should be to you.)

Always take note of anything an editor tells you regarding your novel *whether or not you act on it.* There is always a case for believing so strongly in the novel that you prefer not to change a word and keep trying other publishers.

Sometimes another one will fall upon it with enthusiasm, just as it is. It has happened before. Or you may be so disheartened that all you want to do is fling it to the back of a cupboard. You probably won't want to see it again. *Whatever you do, don't destroy it.*

When you're thinking sanely again, take it out, and try to read it through the editor's eyes. See it as she saw it. See it as Miss Average Romance Reader would see it. As the publisher's experienced reader would have seen it among so many others that she may have read that week.

The novel could still be salvaged with rewriting. Or serve as a guide for future books, on how *not* to write a romantic novel - and in time you'll be able to look on this first one as a useful exercise. You may want to keep the essence of some of the scenes to use in other novels.

But if the real reason for rejection was that it was just a bad novel, don't expect a second or third editor to take pity on you because it's been doing the rounds! If you still get the same reaction from several editors, isn't it time you realised that perhaps they do know what they're talking about after all?

And perhaps your biggest and simplest error was in sending your manuscript out too soon, before you really had a chance to stand back from it and consider it objectively.

New authors are so thrilled that they've actually finished a novel - and rightly so, for that in itself is a comparatively rare achievement - that they pack it up immediately and dash off to the nearest post office without giving it one last critical look, and make those last revisions that could make all the difference to its fate.

However tiny the alterations needed to give the book a final polish, do them. I must confess that I'm not wholly in favour of massive revisions. Nor do I go along with the view popular among some teachers of creative writing that a work will *always* be improved by cutting and honing away. Too much pruning and you'll be left with nothing at all. Your beautiful plant will have withered and died.

I don't believe in getting rid of every adverb and fresh piece of description. I believe more in following your own instincts and writing in *your own style*, not slavishly following someone else's direction. Your own style - what a lovely evocative, important, confidence-building phrase that is - and I don't apologise one iota for that list of adjectives!

Nor do I think that those noble folk who tell you they've rewritten their book six times have necessarily produced a better result than the first draft.

(That's what you're meant to believe, of course, which in turn makes you feel totally inadequate because you only had the patience to rewrite twice.)

Having confessed all, I have to agree that most new writers do tend to over-write and pad. Favourite words or phrases crop up time and again until they become so repetitious that readers are watching out for them and keeping a word-count - and that's the kind of thing you need to revise.

'However tiny the alterations needed to give the book a final polish, do them. I must confess that I'm not wholly in favour of massive revisions.'

But back to the rush to the post office with your precious manuscript. You're not alone. It still happens with published authors. *Believe me, I know!* When that glow of fulfilment is on you, all you want to do is get your fantastic book into someone else's hands, and have *them* tell you how fantastic it is; but please have just a little more patience, if you can. You needed plenty of it to write the book, so a bit more isn't too much to ask, is it?

When you've finished writing your novel, you're still too close to it to be completely objective. If you can bear to put it aside for a few days, or weeks, and then re-read it before submitting it to an editor or agent, those tiny flaws you thought could be overlooked will suddenly show up as glaring mistakes.

It may break your heart to realise you have still more rewriting (however trivial it may seem) to do, but it is worth every extra hour to produce a novel that will have an editor calling you with an offer to publish. Even more heart-stopping than the money she will mention (which can be a pittance or spectacular enough to make you scream with excitement) will be realising that you are on the way to that magical wonderful status you've been yearning for - published author.

Editors are as individual as authors. They have their own views and preferences, but every one of them is looking for the novel with that something extra in it. The Harlequin Mills & Boon guidelines, for instance, have been carefully constructed to elicit the best results from anyone submitting to them, while still allowing the author's originality to show through.

From the moment she looks at your manuscript, an editor becomes a friend. To find a caring editor who will help you through the early stages of becoming a published author, makes you fortunate indeed.

Below are some observations from some well-known editors, and I'm very grateful to them for giving me their comments.

Barbara Boote

Each publisher has a slightly different kind of list, and therefore different requirements and reasons for rejecting manuscripts. There *are* common points: unpublishable because of bad writing, lack of plot, bad dialogue, etc; limitations on the number of books/authors able to be published on a list; similarity of books already bought or commissioned.

Books can be classified into: saga (fatter and more value for money), historical romance (set in an interesting but not overdone period), contemporary romance (shorter and cheaper to sell), and general fiction (must have an angle, realistic background and storyline). One book a year is desirable, and once an author is on a list, it is rare that they are rejected out of hand in the future.

Standards are exceptionally high for first novelists, and a lot of manuscripts are considered marginal and therefore not bought. Some are thought more suitable for a library or hardback readership. A paperback must appeal to a wide range of people.

Rosemary Cheetham

The main reason for rejecting any novel is that, in our opinion, it is simply not good enough. For every novel that we take on, there must be twenty that we reject because they are not well enough written to be publishable. In this context what we mean is that the script has no redeeming features - no lively characters, no realistic dialogue, no vestige of excitement in the story. Among the many people who try their hand at writing fiction, very, very few understand how to tell a story. Even those who plan their novel by writing a synopsis first don't always apply the old rule - that a story must have a beginning, a middle and an end.

The reader must feel satisfied at the end of a novel; all too many first attempts leave one thinking 'So what? What was the point of all that?' You wouldn't dream of standing up at a dinner party and telling a joke which has no punch-line. The same must apply to fiction of all categories. If I had to give two golden rules - plan the story as if it were going to be a television serial, then listen as hard as you can to the way people really talk. The first should give you a page-turning narrative, and the second should provide memorable characters who will live in the reader's mind once that last page has been turned.

'The reader must feel satisfied at the end of a novel; all too many first attempts leave one thinking "So what? What was the point of all that?"'

Diane Pearson

These days there is so much competition for paperback space on the shop bookshelves that anything we publish has to have just that little something extra going for it. We don't publish any series of short category romance, which means that all the romantic novels we do have to earn a unique spot on the list. It doesn't necessarily have to be length or wide canvas: it could be a strong regional background, a truly original storyline, some unusual in-depth characters. Alas, it's no longer possible to accept a competent well-written formula story. Everything has to have a plus.

Maureen Waller

There is nothing so intoxicating for an editor as to find a novel that one wants to publish. A good script stands out as a rare treat. It makes worthwhile all the hours spent negatively reading scripts that will be rejected. It is easier to say why one chooses to publish a certain novel, than to outline the reasons for rejecting others. Quite simply, one has to fall in love with a novel to publish it, and feel impelled to do battle on its behalf through all the various publishing stages, from acquisition to its presentation at the sales conference to the winning of precious review space. The decision to publish is an emotional one as much as a commercial one.

And this is me:

If all the above doesn't prove to you that editors are human too, I don't know what will. We're all aiming for the same thing; to produce a book that readers will eagerly take off the shelves, certain that it's going to be a good, exciting and memorable read. And who knows? It may just be *your* book.

Summing Up

- Try to be objective about your book.

- Take editors' comments into perspective. Note, heed, and decide what to do about them.

- Develop a thick skin and don't take it personally. It's the work that's being evaluated, not you.

- If at first you don't succeed . . . well, you know the answer to that!

Chapter Twelve

Before and After Publication

The last chapter dealt mainly with faults in the writing and construction of your romantic novel. Before it even reaches an editor's desk, you have other things to consider. (Nobody said it was easy).

You may not know how to submit your manuscript. Let's assume that you've now finished your novel and have done whatever revisions were necessary, and are reasonably satisfied that it's ready to be submitted.

You have two options. You can either send it to a literary agent, or direct to a suitable publisher. Acquiring the services of an agent is a personal choice. It can be as hard to find one willing to take on an unpublished author as to sell your book to the publisher. Names and addresses of agents can be found in *The Writers' and Artists' Year Book* or *The Writer's Handbook*, or, better still, through personal recommendation from another author.

Always write a query letter first, telling the agent the kind of novels you write and asking if she/he would be interested in reading your manuscript. Don't give her a sob story about how you're desperate to be published in order to pay the rent. Be professional. Let her see that you're serious about your work, and she'll be more likely to look at it. An agent isn't a writing tutor. She may still return your unpublished manuscript if she truly believes she can't sell it.

She's in business to make money for you and for her. Don't waste her time. If she does take you on, she'll take a percentage of whatever sales she makes on your book - and some publishers will only read manuscripts submitted through an agent.

An advance payment is just what is says. The more money you get to begin with, the longer you have to wait until your book sales have earned out that advance and then you begin to get royalties on it. An advance isn't a gift from the publishers, but a statement on how quickly they think your book will make money. By now, they have a big stake in it too.

For the author who gets a large advance, the publishers may well give that book extra promotion, more sales. If that is the case, then you'll definitely be more inclined to think that your agent has earned her 10 or 15%!

It's essential to have a good rapport with your agent, and to trust her. If those conditions don't exist, get another agent. Remember that she's working for you. But as in all twosomes, communication is important!

I had published six hundred short stories before writing my first contemporary romantic novel. I was advised to send the novel to an agent, which I did, only to be told that *in her opinion* it wasn't publishable. In my opinion, it was. Stubborn? Big-headed? Sometimes you must follow your own instincts, or your own faith in yourself as a writer counts for nothing. So what happened to that first novel?

It didn't go on to the scrap heap. After the tears and depression, I decided to send it out myself. One publisher and then another rejected it, until the fourth one said *YES* - if I would shorten it by 10 percent. It's extraordinarily easy to shorten a novel when you begin to take out all the superfluous passages, and unnecessary bits of dialogue and description - it's easier still with the promise of publication awaiting you. I had revised and retyped within a week.

The result was *Ashton's Folly* (Jean Innes), and that 'unpublishable novel' was published by Robert Hale in 1975 for a very modest advance of £50. It was later published in a Woman's Weekly Library edition, as a Dutch paperback, by Doubleday in America as a hardback book club edition, then as a Bantam US paperback, with sales all over the world.

Eventually it had paid me back thousands of pounds. Not bad for an 'unpublishable novel', that I *might* have thrown to the back of a cupboard - though to be strictly fair, the agent was quite right. As it stood, the novel wasn't publishable. But I include this anecdote as an incentive to all those who have despaired at being rejected by agents and publishers. Take heart. (And no, I will never divulge the name of the agent.)

If you prefer to send your manuscript directly to a publisher, and many successful authors do, you may have already decided on a likely one. Your book may have been tailored to specific needs, such as a Harlequin Mills & Boon, doctor/nurse romance or you'll choose which publisher would be most likely to publish your romantic family saga or whatever.

Either way, don't send your novel to a publisher you've chosen at random. Do your own market research. If you don't, you'll have wasted precious time in launching your career as an author. Your manuscript could come back with coffee stains on it, with ripped corners and with pages missing; you may even find ribald comments from a tough little editor against one of your more romantic and passionate scenes.

These may be extreme examples - but why expect a serious publisher of other genres to waste time on a careless author who can't even sort out a likely publisher for herself?

When you submit to a publisher, include a brief, clear letter, with an outline of the content and category (contemporary romance, saga, romantic suspense, etc). Send either your complete novel, or the first three chapters plus a detailed outline of the book. (Some publishers prefer to see the whole thing, or will only accept a 'partial' when you've had one or more novels taken - see chapter 11.)

Always include sufficient stamps (or International Reply Coupons if appropriate) for return postage. It's good manners, and may speed a reply. If you don't, at the very worst that may be no reply at all, and you will never see your manuscript again. (You do have a copy, don't you?)

Don't ever expect a quick reply, except for an acknowledgement of your manuscript. You should be informed that it's arrived safely, but once you've heard that, then be prepared to wait . . . and wait.

An enormous number of unsolicited manuscripts arrive on editors' desks every week. It takes time to sift through them, send them out to readers, and come to an editorial decision on whether to publish or not. Every novel costs a considerable amount of money to produce, and publishing is a business, not a hobby. The minute you send your novel for consideration by a publisher, you're entering a world of the professionals. Be as professional and efficient as we hope they're going to be!

'When you submit to a publisher, include a brief, clear letter, with an outline of the content and category.'

Any published author will tell you not to sit by the phone or haunt your letter box waiting for news. (They'll tell you, but they all do it.) Forget your masterpiece, if you can, and get on with planning another novel to take your mind off the awful possibility of rejection, or the exhilaration of acceptance, which can be just as traumatic in a different way.

If your novel is accepted, you'll be on a different planet for hours or days or weeks. Never mind if you're asked to do yet more revision by the editor, you'll *do* them, of course. Unless you disagree strongly with the suggestions, in which case politely point out that you'd rather compromise in certain chapters, and hope that she'll agree. It's still your book, so don't be a cabbage! Nor yet a prima donna.

'Any published author will tell you not to sit by the phone or haunt your letter box waiting for news. (They'll tell you, but they all do it.)'

You may be asked out to lunch by the agent and/or editor. You'll meet some of the people who will work on your novel. (You thought you'd already done that?) If word of your success 'somehow' slips out in your town, you may be interviewed by the local newspaper, radio, TV station. All heady stuff. And so far not a word of your novel has been seen by the reading public.

After that, the longest silence you ever knew.

You'll begin to wonder if it was all a dream. You have the contract in your hand, and even though half of it seems written in double Dutch, the agent has vetted it and assures you everything's fine. You've signed it and so has the publisher, but inevitably the first excitement has dwindled, and you start learning what patience is.

It's usually between one and two years before a novel appears in print. Occasionally it's quicker, but it's best to expect later rather than sooner.

Sometime after the first ballyhoo has died down, you will probably get a set of suggested revisions to do. (Not all publishers send them out, but most do.) Argue if you must, but keep in mind that the editor is more experienced in producing a smoothly flowing book than you are. She may just be right!

Your sub-edited manuscript will probably be returned to you at some stage - either before publication for you to keep or dispose of as you will. More likely, you'll be asked to check it electronically on screen. Either way, you'll probably be horrified at the state of it.

Your wonderful novel, that you assumed must be perfect since the publisher bought it and enthused over it, will be a mass of editorial changes, often scribbled in several different coloured pens. Either ignore the corrections to spelling/sentence construction/grammar/over-use of ellipses, etc and use the reverse side of each page for scrap paper, or make good use of the editorial marks to see where your future writing can be tightened. It's an instant lesson in expert revision. Why be foolish enough to ignore it?

But don't just read your book and think how good it is. You're searching for spelling mistakes, missed words, even two sentences transposed, as happened in one of my books.

This is also the last chance for the author to make any alterations to the original manuscript. You *can* add bits or take bits out. But refer back to your contract, and always make corrections with great care. Printers' alterations cost money, and after a certain amount has been spent on them by the publisher, you have to pay the rest! So make as few as possible.

Around this time you may be sent a proof copy of your book jacket. At last you begin to feel like a real author. The jacket is sleek and glossy; the lovers depicted on it look exactly as you imagined (with luck); the title is flamboyant, and your name is there for all to see.

About two weeks before publication day your presentation copies arrive. This is one of the most exciting moments in any author's life. For a first-timer, it's magical. All those months of work, of waiting, of thinking it was never really going to happen, are wiped from your memory.

The book is in your hands at last, and you never thought it would look so beautiful. You have every right to be proud of it. It's an achievement to write a novel. Many, many people start to write one and never finish it. To get a book published at all is even more laudable among so much competition. Don't ever let anyone make you feel otherwise.

Why should they? I hear you say buoyantly, still with your first novel clutched reverently in your hands.

'But it's only a little love story, isn't it, dear . . . it's not real writing, is it?'

The sad thing is that however seriously a romantic author takes her work, creating sincere and intelligent stories, there will always be critics ready to sneer. Remind yourself that you've achieved something they haven't. That you've been considered good enough to be paid for your work.

Then forget the critics, and continue to enjoy doing something that brings its own rewards in personal pleasure and satisfaction.

How many others do you know who do the work they love in the comfort of their own home, and at their own pace? You don't have to write a book in six days or six weeks or six months - unless you tell your publisher that you can and agree to an early delivery date. (If so, live up to it.)

'You've graduated to that wonderful, exciting world of publishing, where anything can happen and sometimes does.'

You've graduated to that wonderful, exciting world of publishing, where anything can happen and sometimes does. A phone call from your agent or your publisher's subsidiary rights department saying your book has sold to an important American publisher can make a bleak winter's day suddenly feel like summer. One of my 'little romances' was condensed as Book of the Month in *Good Housekeeping* magazine in America, Spain and Australia.

Even a lowly paperback sale to an obscure foreign publisher can give you a glow. It may not bring much money, but your name will be on those little plastic-wrapped books on an Italian street bookstall or in some foreign hypermarket, and it will be getting known. And that's what you want - isn't it?

Perhaps you never realised it until the day you're asked to do a book-signing in your local bookshop! It's flattering - and unnerving. You may still be considered an oddity, because you're not a Big Name yet, and because authors *per se* are regarded as somewhat mysterious beings.

'Fancy just sitting down all day doing that!'

Which can make you start to think you're doing something slightly immoral . . .

At a book-signing, be prepared for shoppers to mistake you for a sales assistant. I've sold pens and writing paper and directed people to the record department, despite my books being piled high by my side at my 'signing table'!

It can be fun, as long as you don't take it too seriously, and if it's a success can certainly be good for your ego! But it's even more fun to get back to the real job, which is writing your romantic fiction.

Summing Up

- Present your book as professionally as you can.
- Don't wait by the phone for answers. Get on with writing the next book.
- An agent should always be on your side. If you are not compatible, get another agent.
- Glory in your success when it comes. This is the time to get personal. You've done it!

Chapter Thirteen
Tips from the Top

This chapter is a marvellous lesson in itself for all aspiring authors. Some of our best-known romantic novelists have kindly allowed me to quote them. What comes through is the utter dedication and enthusiasm from all of them. If some of the comments are somewhat similar, I think it only underlines what they have learned through their own efforts.

Heed their advice. But not only that - take note also of the clear and concise way they phrase it. Writing is writing, in whatever guise. So let the experts say it in their own words.

Kate Alexander

I often start my Tilly Armstrong books by thinking of a striking opening sentence and then develop a plot from that. For my Tania Langley and Kate Alexander novels more research and detailed synopses are required. For these I often make a chart and plot the action against world events.

Lists of names (especially of minor characters), dates of birth, physical characteristics, place names, etc can save hours of searching through the manuscript for one elusive fact. I also keep a bibliography, including the library catalogue reference, for rechecking my details.

Tessa Barclay

I'm a great believer in writing an outline before you begin the book. Some writers find this inhibiting, but there's no need to let yourself be bound too rigidly. People who work without one may find characters or development changing so much during the writing that they have to rewrite the beginning.

With a well thought out synopsis, characters and intention are familiar from the outset. An added benefit is that you can see what needs research. You don't have to break off in mid-chapter to find vital facts.

Emma Blair

When I was a young actor one of the first things I learned was that you have to believe absolutely in the character you play on stage, be it drama, comedy or farce. If you don't the audience will realise it and you'll lose them.

It's the same with writing novels, you must believe in the characters you write about, if you don't you'll lose the reader. And characters should be three-dimensional. They have to be living, breathing human beings, not cardboard cut-outs.

Never write about a subject that doesn't interest you; for whatever reasons, it will reflect in the finished work. Every writer has a different approach, but I have always found the best way to keep to a strict routine. This may not be possible for everyone, young mums for example, but it is the method I use and swear by.

Elizabeth Buchan

I do not have any rules, except to write about what currently absorbs and fascinates me. Most novels are concerned with 'the education of the human heart', and human beings do not come wrapped up in formulas, thus I feel strict dos and donts about central characters etc can be rather inhibiting.

The best novels fuse voice, plot and character in such a manner that they continue to engage the reader's imagination after the book is finished. That is what I would like to achieve in my books, and if I manage in the smallest way to do so, then it is all worthwhile.

Barbara Cartland

The secret of writing good romantic fiction is to feel romantic. Unless you believe in true love, which I believe is both spiritual and physical, you will not be a successful writer of this inspiring and divine emotion.

Make your paragraphs not more than three or four lines of print at the outside, which will look like conversation, and be far easier to read. Long paragraphs, to my mind, are only for pedantics! But everything rests, as I have already said, in that you understand the true meaning of the word 'Love'!

Catherine Cookson

Forty-seven years ago, one of the largest correspondence schools in England returned my manuscript without a covering letter, but written across the back page in red ink were the words: 'strongly advise author not to take up writing as a career'. I cried my eyes out; stopped writing for a fortnight; then said to myself:

'What do they know? They have never lived in the north-east of England; they don't know that when I was a girl I was surrounded by famous characters. There was a famous character in every house in our street.'

It is my belief that it isn't the human being acting on the environment that makes the story. It is the environment acting on the human being. The environment is the important factor in the story. Set your environment and the characters will fit into it.

If you touch the heart of a reader, which should be the aim of every writer, then write about the people you know from the inside, then you will get heart into your work. That is what holds the reader. That is what makes one reader say to another those beautiful words: 'I couldn't put it down.'

'The secret of writing good romantic fiction is to feel romantic.'

Barbara Cartland

Jilly Cooper

Get a notebook and allocate about ten blank pages to each of the main characters, then every time you get a thought about one of them, stick it on the relevant pages. That way you build up a dossier about each one, and next time you hear a funny remark one of them might have made, you can put it down immediately before you forget it. I find this very helpful - although I don't always use all that I've filed.

The other thing I have is a second notebook beside me, and hardly a week goes by without my describing what's going on in the countryside - the colour of the trees, what flowers are out, what sunsets are like, what colour the fields are, whether they have been ploughed up.

I find this incredibly valuable because invariably I am so disorganised that I am writing about winter in the middle of the summer, or autumn in the middle of spring, and it's hard to recapture a season unless you've got it written down in front of you. It's also a pleasure to read back later.

Sara Craven

If, like me, you consider yourself the laziest writer in the world, impose the following embargoes on yourself before starting work.

Don't take a look at the crossword/watch breakfast television/phone a friend and ask her for coffee/decide it's a good day for washing curtains.

All those things will be there tomorrow (including the friend). Your fleeting, ephemeral idea may not be. Have a set starting time and adhere to it through flood and fire. Set a daily target of completed script. Exceed it wherever possible.

Margaret Thomson Davis

Don't *say* a character is good or bad, but instead select an incident in which he *shows* himself to be good or bad. Cast him in a dramatic scene. In other words, rather than describe your characters - challenge them!

> '**Don't** *say* **a character is good or bad, but instead select an incident in which he** *shows* **himself to be good or bad.**'
>
> Margaret Thomson Davis

(Excerpt from *The Making of a Novelist* by Margaret Thomson Davis, published by Allison & Busby.)

Natalie Fox

Just do it! Push aside husbands, children and the housework, and just get down to writing your novel. Always write from the heart, because if you are not happy and comfortable with your genre, an editor will know.

Don't be put off by rejections. Think constructive rather than destructive. I had eight novels rejected before I was published, which was very distressing, but I convinced myself that this was my apprenticeship. Each rejection made me more determined to be published, and positive thinking has led to success with twenty-two books published to date.

Iris Gower

Romance in the historical saga must be woven into the plot and brought to life by strong, believable characters. A substantial, well-researched regional backcloth to your novel provides colour and atmosphere and makes for a satisfying read.

Sarah Harrison

Much of the tension of a good love story derives from the obstacles, the prototype being *Romeo and Juliet*. I feel that the true obstacles to romance may be internal, part of the mental and emotional make-up of the protagonists.

Nothing is more poignant than the struggle of two people trying to reach one another who simply do not have the emotional vocabulary to say what they feel. For me, character is everything, and the reader should have the sense of urging the characters on, *willing* them to get together, sometimes in spite of themselves.

Marie Joseph

'Nothing lasts forever, not even love,' Noel Coward said. But cynicism has no part in romantic fiction. We *must* be sincere. If we don't care what happens to our characters, we've lost that vital reader-identification, and our readers won't care either.

Romantic fiction can never be written tongue-in-cheek, so if we don't believe the world to be, well, lost for love, we'd be better off sticking to crime or science fiction, leaving the soaring violins and the moonlight to true romantics.

Elvi Rhodes

'For me, reader-identification is the name of the game, so my storyline is governed by my characters.'
Susan Sallis

My books are historical, so research is important. I *always* spend time in the places I use for my settings. I never write about a place I don't know. I tend to write in scenes, which I see quite clearly in my mind's eye. I put myself in the head of each character taking part. My hope is that this will bring my characters to life, but in any case it's the only way I can work.

Characters are the bedrock of a novel. I like to write about women who are out of the ordinary and get somewhere by their own efforts. They don't have to become rich and famous. They just have to fulfil their dreams and ambitions.

If you're writing your first novel, keep on to the end. You might realise it's not all that good, or suitable for publication, it might make you wince when you look at it years hence. But if you finish it to the proper length you'll know you've overcome a big hurdle. When you start the second one you'll know you can get there. Now you can concentrate on doing it better.

Susan Sallis

For me, reader-identification is the name of the game, so my storyline is governed by my characters. They can change things simply by being themselves. In other words, once I've 'caught' them, they are in charge, and if I ask them to do things they wouldn't dream of doing, they let me know.

A sleepless night ensues (for me), followed by a morning consultation (with them) and, I hope, we get back on the right track. Romantic novels are about two people falling in love. My advice is - get to know them.

Jessica Stirling

The best scenes of romantic and sexual encounter (where my characters finally get to rub noses) are invariably written in a kind of exultation, fingers fair flying over the keyboard. But, and this is the point, they aren't left that way. The heat of creative composition fires the writing, certainly, but it's cold-blooded revision and reworking that adds sureness and certainty of touch.

Learning how to revise intelligently, without smothering the initial 'fire', is where craftsmanship and experience really come into play. It takes time and effort to learn how to do this well, so don't be impatient (or lazy) when it comes to editing your breathless prose. Therein can lie the difference between finding a publisher eager to take your novel, and not finding a publisher at all.

Reay Tannahill

I have a suspicion that Rule 1 for aspiring novelists - 'Write about what you know' - was coined by someone who had been taught always to think positively. A mistake, in this case, because although familiarity may lend assurance, it doesn't do much to stimulate the imagination. And it's imagination that puts the spark in all fiction worth reading, whatever the genre.

Rule 1, in fact, makes better literary sense (common sense, too) when put negatively, viz. '*Don't* write about something you *don't* know'. So if you fancy writing about other lives, other places, other times, go ahead. *Get* to know them and you'll be very unlucky indeed if, in the process, you don't find your imagination excited by all the things that are fresh and new to you. Which ought, at the very least, to get your book off to a flying start.

Joanna Trollope

I always feel that the popularity of romantic fiction is proof of how admirably ambitious women are about relationships - they *always* feel things could be better, and they're right! For this reason alone, I think the writing of romantic fiction must always be taken seriously, but never solemnly.

The research - past or present - must be meticulous and as invisibly used in the text as you can. The characters must be true to their period - no post-Freudian behaviour for pre-Freudian people - and as unstereotypical as possible.

There should be tension, to keep the reader turning the pages; there should only be the amount of sex interest that you, the writer, truly feel comfortable with (romance extends way, way beyond the bedroom); and there should *always* be humour.

Mary Wibberley

Don't rewrite too many times and take all the life out of your book. There is a lovely freshness in a first writing that is destroyed by constant alterations. Do only what is necessary.

Don't be timid. Be yourself. You are unique. No one has ever said or written before *exactly* what you are saying or writing. The world may be waiting to hear *you*. Be bold. Go ahead and say it. You've nothing to lose but an inferiority complex.

Do read a lot in-between writing your books. You will be delving into other writers' minds, drawing on the rich store of imagination - you will *be* part of the wonderful world of books.

Excerpt from *To Writers With Love* by Mary Wibberley, published by Buchan & Enright.)

Summing Up

- Take heed of what published authors say. They made it.

- Endless tinkering will take the freshness out of your book. Revise enough, and no more.

- Be original and develop your own style. It is unique to you, and no one else does it quite like you.

- Keep going and don't be deterred by adverse criticism, nor seduced by too much praise.

Need2Know

Chapter Fourteen
Let's be Practical

I consider the previous chapter to be an invaluable collection of quotations. You will not agree with all of them. You may find some of their views conflicting, not only among the authors, but with some of the points I have made, and with what you inherently believe yourself.

Showing that these successful writers have sometimes forceful and conflicting ideas proves the point that there is no hackneyed formula in romantic fiction writing. Each author, and therefore each book, is an individual, and developing your own voice and style is one of the great assets of any writer.

Even if you disagree strongly with anything you've read so far, it's still a useful exercise to take note of those writers who are successfully published in the genre in which you yourself want to write. This is a highly competitive market, and, after all, they made it.

You cannot have missed the fact that the overall concept of writing romantic and historical fiction covers many areas. Within the quotations from those successful authors, you will have gleaned details of the various types of novels that the terms 'romance' and 'romantic fiction' embrace.

If you're still confused as to what is right for *you*, then some explanation of the divisive categories within the genre might be useful. You might still be unsure as to what may be your particular writing niche, and I emphasise again that publishers do attempt to categorise every novel they publish, if only to give it a selling hook. We may not like it, but they do.

So this chapter deals in more detail with just what each term that you see on the spine of a published novel, or in a publisher's catalogue, means. Starting with the most obvious one of all . . .

> 'You cannot have missed the fact that the overall concept of writing romantic and historical fiction covers many areas.'

Contemporary romance

It should be self-explanatory, but pay attention to that word 'contemporary', and keep your characters and settings up to date. All avid readers of contemporary romance expect to read a story of *today,* in that strange ever-present timing of this kind of book. It means being up to date on slang, for instance. Use it in moderation because it changes so quickly. Nothing dates a contemporary novel more than reading words that were fashionable ten years ago. (Unless that is your intention, of course.)

Similarly with twee phrases and cosy situations. And avoid having every heroine's parents die conveniently in a car crash before the story begins. It may well happen with depressing frequency in real life, but in fiction it becomes a contrivance if it crops up too often.

There is contemporary and contemporary. Some novels are definitely on the 'sweet' side, and would appeal more to older readers who still yearn for the good old days of fiction reading (and why should they be bombarded with scenes to make them blush if they prefer the milder type of romance?). I've said it before - give them a good storyline and characters who really care about one another. You'll satisfy your gentle readers, and your editor too - providing you've researched your market and know where to send your book. (No, I'm not going to list publishers and requirements in detail. You have to do *some* of the work for yourself!)

Spicier contemporary novels use a different technique. Here, the accent is on wringing every ounce of sexual tension out of every situation between your lovers, and being unafraid to let them have their gloriously uninhibited love scenes - but for heaven's sake, don't let it read like a series of sex scenes and nothing else. A good storyline is still essential. Your story must be going somewhere, otherwise it's not a story at all.

Gothic/Romantic suspense

I've put these two categories together, but there are differences as well as similarities. The old Gothic novel used to be everybody's favourite reading. It fell out of fashion some time back but, as always, fashions change, and it frequently appears again in a slightly different guise. Write a good enough book, and somebody will want to publish it.

The Gothic novel is one where the heroine is in danger from the outset of the book. An old house with lots of atmosphere is often involved, and comes over as almost another 'character' because of its importance. Gothics frequently have wild, isolated or mysterious settings, such as Cornwall, the Scottish Highlands, or the Yorkshire moors.

The heroine is never quite sure until the end which of two charismatic men is the hero and which is the villain. I used this technique in my book *The Devil's Kiss* (Sally Blake) and in *Blackmaddie* (Rowena Summers). The two men in the books are both charming in different ways . . . In this type of novel the author's skill lies in *almost*, but not quite revealing to the reader which is the villain until the last moment . . . and here it's essential that the hero's qualities have the edge over the villain's. The reader must never end up wishing your heroine had got the other one!

When the inevitable (but logical) conclusion is reached and the hero saves the heroine from disaster at the eleventh hour, the little clues the author has inserted throughout the book suddenly become crystal clear.

Usually, the hero will be explaining some of them to the still doubting, half dead/drowned/demented but ever-resilient heroine! Since most Gothics are very dramatic, they're usually historical novels. Victoria Holt's novels are excellent examples.

Romantic suspense is the modern equivalent of the well-tried Gothic, but in a contemporary setting. These are trickier to write to make them plausible, but if you can do it, and bring the tension and excitement to your writing that the genre demands, then good luck!

Women in jeopardy

This is the popular in-name for what could be labelled a mixture of the Gothic novel and romantic suspense, but in a more modern setting. Again, the heroine is in some highly dangerous situation, but the elements producing it will be far more contemporary. She will also be more capable of dealing with the traumas herself than in an old-style situation where she played the helpless female at the mercy of whatever ills befell her. A strong heroine is essential for this kind of novel, to combat all the troubles you put her way.

Nostalgia

I'm inventing the label for this category, to include all the marvellous novels that conjure up events from the First World War onwards. Three of my novels which come into this category are *All in the April Morning*; *The Bannister Girls*; and *To Love and Honour*.

Nostalgia novels include wartime romances, romances set between the wars, and even romances in the 1950s and 1960s which can still make us sigh a little for times past . . . Don't we all love to dream over days that are gone? We all look back and see things through rose-coloured glasses. So when you write of those days, write from the heart, with that extra touch of poignancy, remembering the love and the laughter and the dangers we shared.

But get your facts right! Research should always be accurate, and although it's tempting to think that you can remember things that time has mellowed in your mind, your readers may remember facts more clearly than you do! So double-check them. Especially fashions in clothes and music. Don't mistakenly substitute some of the favourite songs of the forties for the twenties! The world is ever-changing and so are the people in it. Make yours live and breathe in the era you put them in.

Regional novels

These can be contemporary or historical, but recently the regional historical novel has definitely grown in popularity. There's a special kind of appeal in writing about your own locality. Since every novel is local to someone, why make such a song and dance about it, you may ask? Well, I write regional novels as Rowena Summers, and I believe they work because I write about places I know well. I tend to think of the entire West Country as my region, and I think that we all have a special empathy with our own locality. It becomes part of us, and we become part of it.

By delving into the history of your own area, you will almost certainly come up with a wealth of background material for a novel. And because you can combine your research with your own knowledge of the land and the people, you will write your book with an insight that another author from 'outside' may miss. I feel strongly that this is true. Readers of Catherine Cookson's novels, for instance, instantly see themselves, or people like themselves, from her marvellous descriptions of Tyneside.

Period novels

Not quite such a demand these days as there used to be for the gentle type of historical novel that doesn't seem to fall into any particular genre, except that its characters exist in some vague Victorian setting, frequently with the lady's companion as its heroine. To do well, it all comes back to the kind of treatment you put on the book, and on your own style. Make it readable, and who knows? You may just be starting the next reading fashion. Readers still love them, and some authors still stick rigidly to the old favourite period novel. Few enough that they have captured their own little corner of the market. That can't be bad, can it?

Regency

The vogue for Regencies comes and goes but never dies. Someone somewhere always seems keen to publish these delightful, frothy historical novels set in a period that spanned no more than a few decades. Georgette

'By delving into the history of your own area, you will almost certainly come up with a wealth of background material for a novel.'

Heyer's name immediately comes to mind whenever Regency novels are mentioned. A new author could do no better than to study her books to get the feel and flavour of the Regency, and then read some of the contemporary authors who write them with such flair. Sheila Walsh won the Romantic Novelists' Association's Major Award in 1984 for her Regency novel entitled *A Highly Respectable Marriage* (Hutchinson). What a wonderfully evocative title for that particular kind of book. Readers know what to expect and are rarely disappointed. Regencies have a wit and style all their own, and it may just be that that's the opening that's right for you.

Note. American publishers are particularly keen on Regency novels, and many other sub-genres. The next chapter deals in depth with the lucrative American romance market.

Aga-sagas

This sub-genre surged to popularity several years ago, and it is anybody's guess how long the trend for it will continue. The term comes from an old-style cooking range seen in modest homes, which then became a kind of status symbol for well-heeled country-dwellers. So the stories themselves reflect this background and scenario. They involve middle-class characters living the comfortable life, and the books are generally considered more upmarket in tone and content than some of the other genres.

Sagas

This is my favourite category. My favourite to read and to write, and that's something to think about when you first decide which sort of book you want to tackle. You may not know at first. I didn't. I began writing short stories for women's magazines before I really knew that I wanted to write novels. Even then, I wasn't sure which kind. I wrote a teenage novel, a contemporary romance and a short historical romance.

Whichever one I sold, I decided to follow that road. Eventually they all sold, and I wrote all three types for some time. Then it dawned on me that what I really wanted was to write long books, books that I could get my teeth into as a writer, and which I could feel most satisfaction in producing.

If you think that brief résumé of my writing career makes it sound incredibly easy, I assure you it was not. I am as familiar with rejection letters as anyone, but right from the beginning I was determined to succeed and nothing was going to put me off. I was also very lucky - and still am - in having a husband who backed me all the way.

When I was a child, I thought that 'being a writer' was the most glamorous and exciting profession in the world. I 'practised' even then by writing little plays for the neighbours' kids to perform. It amazes me how often other authors say the same thing. (Perhaps I should retract my words in the introduction about born writers.)

I still think it's the most exciting profession, only now I know how much dedication and hard work goes into it. I've always had a love affair with words, with the evocative phrases and patterns that they make, and I've never lost my enthusiasm - and the more enthusiasm you put into your writing, the more vivid your work will be. It will lift your story out of the ordinary and carry your readers along with it.

So what has my own 'writing saga' to do with the saga?

Saga writing is dearest to my own heart, and because by its nature it deserves more space, I wanted to convey some of my own drive to you. When people ask me where I get my energy, I can only say that I have it because I love my work, and writing sagas is what I love most of all. The planning of a big novel is like being on the brink of an exciting journey, with all the characters assembling and joining the train/ship/plane at different times and each becoming part of the whole.

When readers pick up that big book to take home, they are deliberately choosing a novel that is likely to give them days or weeks of reading pleasure. A novel with twists and turns, with characters that not only come alive on the page, but who grow and develop and change *because of the time-span of the book*. As the author of a saga, you will, of course, give your characters a logical reason for every changing opinion that occurs.

The most familiar type is the family saga. Aim to draw your reader as quickly as possible into the family you create, so that she thinks of them as her own. The saga plot is intricate and detailed, which is what makes it so fascinating to

'When readers pick up that big book to take home, they are deliberately choosing a novel that is likely to give them days or weeks of reading pleasure.'

write and to read. It's a continuing soap opera. It has many interweaving sub-plots, and something of interest is always happening because a saga must have page-turning qualities to make it magical.

Family sagas - who hasn't read one? You know you're in for a good read as soon as you get the gist of it from the blurb on the jacket. Every one of us can identify with family happenings. It all comes back to that good old stand-by, reader-identification.

Some family sagas cover one person's life from cradle to grave, or, more often, old age. Some sagas cover only one year. The changing seasons in, say, a rural setting can give the illusion of a much longer time-span. The one-year period gives you a tight framework to work to, especially when dealing with country pursuits.

Back to the family. There's an enormous wealth of material to be drawn from it. A family is never just a family. Think of any you know. Your own, or one in the public eye, the royal family, perhaps. Think of the differences in its members, their physical appearances, mental abilities, political views, strengths and weaknesses.

A second marriage within a family can result in great differences in the children, creating rivalry and grudges, jealousy and competitiveness. Or treachery, where one brother is more power-mad than another or when one sister wants her sister's man. There can be incest.

Having mentioned all the nasty characteristics within families, let's not forget the plus side. The closing-in of the family when outsiders threaten any one of them. That peculiar bond of loyalty that says that blood is thicker than water. There's the intense sadness within a family, not only from bereavement, but when one member breaks away. In a tight-knit community, it was once a major calamity when one person wanted to leave the home environment. All these permutations and many more can be used when working out your characters for a family saga.

This is the perfect time for working out their family tree. Immediately you do so, in some miraculous way all these people will become real to you. And don't forget that in a saga you can give your characters any medical or mental peculiarities you wish. With the large cast of characters that a long book must have, there's bound to be a variety of ailments that you can exploit.

Many of the points in chapter 9 about weaving fictional characters with real ones are especially valid in writing historical sagas.

But not all sagas are about families. The theme can be a power-struggle, male or female. The desire for power can be as potent as any drug, and the obsessive hero or heroine can be a very strong central character. Survival sagas where a character defies all the odds to emerge triumphant always make an emotional and powerful read.

A saga is written in many layers or levels, and sometimes you'll want to liven up the action by bringing in a new character. Providing he's relevant to the plot, that's fine.

He may in fact leave the story after his significant scenes or chapters, but he will have made his mark, in some way have been a catalyst to some definite twist of the plot. All your sub-plots must link in some way. If they don't, cut them out.

Readers love continuity in novels, and the saga is the ideal way of producing it. It's a thrill when a favourite author writes a sequel to a novel. It's even more of a thrill to the author when you realise you've got the potential for a sequel - or more. This happened with my *Killigrew Clay* (Rowena Summers). It began as one book, set in the Cornish china-clay industry, then became a trilogy, and eventually became a sequence of eight novels following the same family from the 1850s until the end of the second world war.

It's lovely to know your background and your characters, and not have to say goodbye to them at the end of the book after all, because they'll be coming back.

If you've got the stamina and inspiration to write a lengthy novel, then why not try a saga? I guarantee that you'll enjoy it. For me, there's romance in the very word.

Rachel Moore is my pen name for writing wartime sagas set in Cornwall during the Second World War. The dangers and heartbreaks of wartime, the partings and reunions, give an added dimension of tension and drama to any novel in which relationships are constantly under stress.

Summing Up

- Write the book you would like to read.

- Sweet romance or dramatic historical?

- Sagas take stamina and dedication, but in the end you'll have a satisfying big book.

- Always get emotionally involved with your characters. Their problems will wring it out of you, but that's good!

Chapter Fifteen

The American Romance Market

The American romance market is a very important one to British authors. Simply because of the size of the country, the supply and demand for books is much larger than in Britain.

While it's one thing for a British author to sell American paperback rights to a book that's done well here, to go straight in and offer an unpublished manuscript to a big American publisher who's probably never heard of you, is far more of a gamble. And *if you don't give them what they want,* they're not going to buy your book.

I've written many novels for the American romance market, both contemporary and historical. Some have been originals, written specially for American publishers, and some have been editions of books that were published here. So what sells, and what doesn't?

American romance readers look for novels with plenty of pace, action and movement in the story. They don't like slow, long, drawn-out beginnings, and you should not only aim to get your characters on stage very early on in the first chapter, but also to set up the problems they're going to encounter as soon in the novel as is feasible.

Readers will expect to identify with the heroine, so introduce her on page one, and let the reader know her mood of the moment as soon as you can. This probably sounds like familiar advice to anyone writing romantic fiction, and so it is. There's not much difference in British and American romance when it comes to the basics of getting the characters on stage early, giving them conflict and problems in their relationship, which are going to be resolved by the end of the book.

Characters' moods

It's surprising how many people forget to establish the mood of the main character at the beginning of the book. We all have different moods, and your chapter one may begin, for instance, when your basically sane and sensible heroine is in a state of high old excitement at learning that she's won a fortune, or whatever. Your writing should convey that mood right away, so that you involve your readers in that excitement.

So if she's about to make a career move, or go somewhere to collect a legacy, or change her entire lifestyle for some reason, don't spend six pages waffling on about her early life that led up to this point. The important thing in the book is *now*, so don't wander further into the past than you have to, at least not at the beginning. There's always time enough later for filtering in all the background information that's necessary.

'Your characters don't have to be American unless any guidelines specifically state as much.'

Your characters don't have to be American unless any guidelines specifically state as much. This is something that can put people off attempting to write a book for this market. But if you can write about American characters authentically, why not? And with all the US TV programmes on our screens, you can adequately research the way Americans speak and behave.

Obviously if you travel there, you will learn all this at first-hand. Having an American penfriend can be an enormous help as well, if only for finding out such little details as how much it costs to make a phone call, or the prices of motel rooms, or the names of the most used stores and fast-food restaurants etc. (They're not all McDonald's.)

American romance publishers are never afraid to try something new, and novels dealing in depth with sensitive subjects such as alcoholism or drug abuse, or even child abuse, can be included as long as these subjects are handled well, with a caring relationship being part of the plot.

Despite the more emotionally-charged subject matter, it does make a refreshing change from the novels that were always so sugary sweet, and rarely dealt with any realistic problems. Topical themes, such as caring for the environment, or trying to prevent commercial excavations destroying an historical site, for instance, would certainly fit as a background.

Focal point of romances

As a general rule, the longer the novel, the more freedom you have in exploring wider issues but, as in all romantic fiction, always remember that the romance between the two central characters must remain the focal point of the novel, otherwise you might as well be writing something else.

A romantic novel, on either side of the Atlantic, is not a sex manual, nor a treatise on wine-growing, a travelogue or a sailing guide. But many readers do enjoy and expect informative details about the setting and/or occupations of the characters. So there must be at least enough details for the reader to identify in which part of the world the action is taking place, and more importantly, *why* the characters are there.

Give your characters motivation for everything they do. And credit your readers with intelligence enough not to be fobbed off with a weak plot where the characters do nothing but meander through the pages. Such books simply won't sell.

Romantic clichés

Although you should try to avoid all the so-called romantic clichés mentioned earlier in this book, unfortunately they still form the phrases used on the blurbs of many American novels, even when the authors avoid writing them. You may feel brave enough to object to the style of the blurb - or offer to write it yourself - or just grit your teeth and take the money. But remember that the publishers will have done their homework, and will know what appeals to their readership.

Many of the things that apply to the more British-based Harlequin Mills & Boon romances also apply to the American market, not only for the American parent company, Harlequin Books, but to American publishing as a whole. There should be plenty of action and dialogue, and the hero and heroine should be on stage together as much as possible, avoiding long absences between them. There are many ways in which the hero can still be in the heroine's mind, even when they're apart, as you'll have read earlier in this book. They apply equally well to American romantic fiction.

One of the differences in our two cultures is the enthusiasm with which the keenest American romance readers will buy their books by the armful. I've seen them at supermarket checkouts in the States, buying the current six or eight Silhouette Romances at one time. The women who buy them in that way are obviously the most avid romance readers, and for the writer to succeed in that market, you *have* to be prepared to give them what they want to read. They're buying romance novels, with the emphasis on romance, so don't skimp on the love scenes.

In general, American fictional love scenes are not only more sensual, but they also extend over more pages, than in most British fiction. Of course, this all depends on the publisher, and the particular type of books you're writing. It's certainly not obligatory to put in a love scene every twenty pages or so. Your strong, passionate characters should dictate when a love scene should occur, and just how passionate it is.

'Don't use words like "sidewalk" and "elevator", unless the book has an American setting.'

Love scenes will generally be undeniably sexy, or filled with sexual tension. The novels rarely include rape, although the heroine is sometimes threatened by it, and she is only ever romantically involved with the hero. In the historical novels, in particular, she is very romantically involved with him. This is what readers expect, and what you need to give them if you want to be published in the lucrative American market.

The publishers are not squeamish about the clinches and the explicitness of the descriptions of *what's going on* - though in no way does it compare with the descriptions in erotic novels. Sex in American historical romance lines is certainly titillating, and is meant to be, without detailed, clinical description. These books aren't classed as erotica, and the strong romantic element is always uppermost.

General tips

Don't use words like 'sidewalk' and 'elevator', unless the book has an American setting. If the book takes place in nineteenth-century England, with English characters, for instance, it would be a mistake to call a pavement a sidewalk, just to please an American editor, because it would simply sound wrong. American publishers are keen on British history, and if you can bridge the two countries through your characters and plots, so much the better.

Need2Know

Historical romances that take place anywhere in the world stand as good a chance as any, providing they contain a good, fast-moving story. My various historicals have backgrounds of Africa, Scotland, England, a fictional Greek island, Australia, the gold-fields of California, Egypt, Cyprus and Ireland.

To be successful in the American *contemporary* romance market, your fictional heroines should reflect the way that American women look at life; which is positively and confidently, and many of the readers will be career-orientated themselves. You only have to watch any of their TV shows to know the almost frightening confidence that some of them have.

Romantic heroes are never wimps, nor impossibly rude and arrogant as they used to be in fiction some years ago, and this is also a refreshing change for the better. The more vulnerable hero has come into favour, and he often has an Achilles heel that only the heroine can find. This could be something like the hero having had a poor early life that makes him ruthless in business, or a decision never to marry because of some flaw in his parents' marriage, or seeing the marriages of too many close friends fail. The heroine will be the one who will eventually change his mind over all that, of course.

If you use a situation like the one I've just described, you would have to be careful not to make the hero seem to cling too much to the past. You must make him appear strong-willed enough to deal with and overcome his problems through his own motivation. With a little help from the heroine, of course.

American men, on the whole, are extremely polite to women. Note this trait on TV films or soap operas. Even in the heavier cops and robbers stuff, you will find they call women 'ma'am' and other men 'sir', which is something we rarely do in such a natural way here, but it happens in real life too. You needn't overdo this trend in your novels, but when you read a lot of American romantic fiction, you find that this general politeness is reflected in the attitudes of men to women in the books.

The theme of your novel should have more depth than just 'love conquers all'. The way your two main characters meet, and the reasons for their outer conflicts and inner problems, should all play a part. In contemporary novels, the heroine in American romances will probably have an interesting career, which in some way mirrors the type of woman you're writing for. The days when

'American men, on the whole, are extremely polite to women. Note this trait on TV films or soap operas.'

she can merely be a travelling companion to some vague elderly relation are long gone. She can be anything you care to make her, from an airline pilot to a mechanic, a doctor, a specialised teacher, or the boss of a huge company.

Keep in mind that you are writing an intelligent romance about intelligent characters, with a background that you're either familiar with, or can research well enough to make the heroine's job seem believable. Don't overload the book with technical details of her work, but give enough of the flavour of it for readers to know that this is a woman who is perfectly capable of dealing with her own life.

However successful in her professional life you make your heroine, she still needs to be feminine enough to make her irresistible to the hero. And we all know that there's absolutely no reason why brains and beauty can't go together. This very fact has been the start of many a conflict between hero and heroine, when he arrives at a new job expecting to see a male director of operations, and finds an attractive woman in charge instead.

When you describe scenery, put your characters into that scenery and let it be seen through their eyes. I can't stress often enough that the ability to write visually is one of the great assets of writing successful fiction, in any genre. In the same way, if you describe some industry, artistic or sporting activity, it must belong to the book because one of the characters is involved in it. Don't throw in sidelines of research information just to pad out the pages.

Be careful about letting one character explain the workings of some detailed technical machinery to the other. You may well need to do this to establish the working relationship and technology aspects of your book, but do it in small doses, otherwise it can come across as a bit of clever author research thrown in for the reader to admire. (She'll admire it anyway.)

Publishers' guidelines

Many American publishers issue guidelines. These are an enormous help in defining the settings, ages and generalities of your characters. But if you follow these guidelines too closely your book may turn out to be a clone of every other book on the bookshelves. If you don't want to write, or send, the entire manuscript at once, most publishers will give you an opinion on the first three chapters and synopsis, and some will commission the book on this basis. This saves you postage but takes up time while you're waiting for an opinion. Not all publishers take kindly to multiple submissions, ie sending the same three chapters and synopsis to several publishers, although most are now more accepting of this practice. It certainly saves time, because if one publisher turns the book down, you hope to have several more copies elsewhere.

If you want to send a manuscript or partial manuscript to several publishers at the same time, always state in the covering letter that you're sending it as a multiple submission, and that you'll inform the editor at once if you get an offer for the book. This is perfectly acceptable and, if they want your book, they'll usually phone you to make an offer and discuss the contract rather than sending a letter.

What about the sheer cost of sending a manuscript to America? This is obviously avoided if you have an agent, but for those who don't, it's not cheap. Sending it by air mail means including International Reply Coupons, and is by far the safest method, since sending it by sea mail can take forever. You don't have to have an agent to submit novels to US publishers as they're quite happy to look at typescripts sent direct from authors.

If you travel to the States, and have a book ready, take it with you and post it from there, which is much cheaper. But first, remember that if an American publisher does decide to buy your book, it will have been well worthwhile spending the money on postage. Since the country is vast, your sales will far outdo any that you get in Britain. Even if royalties are very low in some cases, such as the home book club subscription books, the quantities sold will still give you a healthy income.

You can find many American publishers' addresses simply by looking around our own bookshops. We get a lot of American paperback imports, and the address of the publishing house can be found inside the front cover. A list of the most popular ones is also included at the end of this book. It's definitely worth reading the books to see what American publishers are currently buying. You may not care for the jackets they use, and some of them are quite lurid, which leads the reader into thinking that the books are all about sex.

American romance readers certainly like their quota of sexy reading, but it all depends on the book you're writing, the type of characters you're writing about, and the publisher you're aiming for. If you're unhappy at writing explicit scenes, there are plenty of lines where you don't need to go into great detail, although sexual tension should always be present between the hero and heroine in a romantic novel.

You may have the title of your book changed to suit their particular line and, unless it really hits the mark for their list, it will probably be changed for a title that's far more exotic than the one you chose. It's up to you if you think this is worth making an issue about.

The main organisation in America for romantic fiction authors is the Romance Writers of America. For your current sub plus airmail postage rates, you receive a bi-monthly magazine. There are always articles written by authors, agents and so on, and it is very good value for money for anyone seriously wanting to get into the American romance market.

The organisations hold an annual conference in a different US city each year. It now has nearly 8,000 members, the majority of whom are not yet published, and more than 1,700 of them attended the most recent conference that I attended in New York City. Many publishers and agents attend and, as well as talks by these people and by authors, one of the most useful aspects for unpublished writers at these conferences is the one-to-one editor/author appointments. Most of the talks are taped so that people can buy or order them at a later date.

Publishers aren't averse to humour in your characters, and witty dialogue between hero and heroine is fine, as long as it doesn't descend into slapstick. The humour also has to be integral to a character's make-up, and not thrown in for the sake of it, any more than an extraneous sex scene should be thrown in every twenty pages or so. Both should occur naturally, because of the way you have created your characters.

Laughter can create a wonderful bond between two people, and passion needn't always be a serious business. Lust can also be fun. Give your hero a sense of humour too. Rhett Butler had a sense of humour in *Gone with the Wind* and the ultra-dour, broodingly silent types went out with Heathcliff.

Since emotional content should be very high on the agenda when writing a romance, pathos also has its place, providing it doesn't become maudlin. This extra appeal to the emotions especially applies to the big historical novel, where you will almost certainly have more deaths and disasters to deal with than in the shorter contemporary romance. But shorter length and few characters shouldn't mean a lack of emotion, or you'll end up writing a one-dimensional story.

It's impossible to try to generalise about an entire race, but in the number of times I've been to America, I've found people to be emotional, volatile, extremely warm and friendly, for whom nothing is too much trouble. You are catering for these people as readers, so remember to make them laugh, make them cry, but never let them be bored. Aim to carry your readers along with visual and vigorous writing, and make them really care what happens to your characters.

Contracts and sales

A final word about contracts. American contracts cover most of the same ground as British ones, but are far longer and more detailed. Some of the library publishers pay fairly modest advances, but in general the advance you can expect to get for a paperback romance novel may be $3,000, or much more, but this will depend on the publisher and the author's status, and I can only generalise. Royalties are usually paid at six percent, sometimes rising, depending on the number of copies sold.

It's quite usual for authors to be given a multi-book contract once they've become established, and this is not the same as the option clause in a contract, where a publisher asks for the first option on your next novel. A multi-book contract means that they are offering an overall advance, for, say, three books, and you'll be paid one-third, or one-half, of the total sum on signing the contract, then a proportion of the remainder as each completed book is delivered.

The thought of a multi-book contract can be unnerving as well as exciting, as they may only have seen the first book, or even only the first proposal, and you're then committed to write several more that are just as acceptable. But since this doesn't normally happen until they know you're capable of giving them what they want, you don't need to worry about it until you have the first sale under your belt.

Sales obviously do far exceed those in Britain, and you usually receive twenty-five free copies of your book from American publishers, instead of the six or twelve that British publishers give.

There are outlets for almost every kind of romance novel in America except doctor/nurse books, which don't sell well over there. They publish ethnic romance, mystery romance, sci-fi romance, paranormal romance, adventure romance, as well as the more traditional kinds of contemporaries and historicals. There's a lot of scope for Regencies right now, but not much demand for Gothics. British writers can succeed in this enormous market for well-researched, pacy books that tell a real story about strong and appealing characters. Why not you?

Summing Up

■ Avoid using romantic clichés. They're old-hat and irritating to read.

■ Keep up the pace in your book and don't let it flag by unnecessary padding.

■ Make your love scenes believable. Once readers start to cringe, you've lost them.

■ People are people, whatever their background.

Chapter Sixteen

Further Help

Some people find it easy to learn from manuals. Others need the personal contact of a teacher. Actually finishing the writing of a romantic or historical novel can seem an impossible task for someone who has never attempted it before, even though it's falsely assumed to be so easy. If you've been unsuccessful so far, you'll know that it's not that simple, and often an encouraging word from someone who's been there is worth its weight in gold.

Even so, my personal view and the advice given by other authors in this book still give the beginner no guarantee of success. Nothing will do that but the spark within each author, the sincere love of this kind of fiction, the talent, and the drive to continue against all the odds.

Writing is a solitary career. Some call it lonely. It depends on what you understand by that word. I'm never lonely when I'm involved with my fictional people, but I would strongly advise against cutting yourself off from the outside world in your wish to be published.

Other people can trigger the ideas for interesting characters for your book. Other writers can be the inspiration that lifts you out of rejection blues to the determination that if they can do it, so can you! A sympathetic word from someone who knows the traumas of waiting for the editor's reply, and who understands the misery of beginning all over again, is worth a great deal.

'Some people find it easy to learn from manuals. Others need the personal contact of a teacher.'

Writing classes

If you have no 'writing friends' living near you - and few of us do when we begin - then what can you do? There are innumerable sources from which to draw further help. You could enrol at a local writing class in your area. But be prepared to find that it may just be filled with fringe-type 'writers' who think it's a bit 'arty' to write, in which case you may feel you're getting no real help.

If that's so, forget it. A writers' class whose members provide little more than a mutual admiration society is worse than useless, for you'll just end up having a false idea of your own work. Editors aren't so ready to give praise where none is due, because that's not their job. But their criticism will be more useful to you in the end than that of well-meaning friends.

If you're lucky, you may live in an area where there is one of the marvellous writers' classes that offer real help and encouragement - they do exist and are usually organised by the WEA or Local Education Authority. Its members will be studying the craft in the same spirit as you are - with the compulsion to write and be published. (Your local library will have details of evening classes.)

'A writers' class whose members provide little more than a mutual admiration society is worse than useless, for you'll just end up having a false idea of your own work.'

You'll be mixing with people who know what you mean when you speak of 'writer's block' and royalty statements and the pros and cons of agents. Their eyes won't glaze over when you try to describe how you 'see' your characters and how difficult it is to research some seemingly simple fact, such as when the word 'scrumpy' was first used to mean Somerset cider, a problem I was once faced with.

Creative writing courses

You think that a weekly class is not for you? Then consider going away on a creative writing course. Those who have attended such working weekends will tell you of their immense value. Libraries may be able to help with information on them, or you can find details in general publications for writers such as *Writers' Forum, Writers' News* and *Writing Magazine,* etc (See Appendix 1).

These and other writers' magazines also offer excellent articles on all aspects of writing, and most of them include current market requirements. Subscribing to one or more, you will discover you're not working in the void you may have believed. There are many more aspiring authors like you, wondering where to seek constructive help. Suddenly you are not alone.

Postal tuition is another possibility, and there are reputable postal schools, which advertise in writing magazines. Some courses are general ones, and the advice on romantic or historical fiction is only a small proportion of their prospectus. So look for one that caters for your own writing needs.

Many authors have found that the most valuable conference of all is the Writers' Summer School, held every August in Swanwick, Derbyshire. www. swanwickwritersschool.co.uk

Six days of intensive 'writing' talk with more than three hundred other devotees, with lectures and discussion groups and specific courses, informal chats between top professional authors and complete beginners; all combine to make up an exciting, heady mixture, and at the end of it all, most people go home determined to come back next year with at least something published!

You will discover another bonus, I have found writers to be the most warm and generous people I know in giving their time and advice and friendship in the creative world we share. From knowing 'no one', I now have countless 'writing' friends, and I love them all.

Writers' organisations and prizes

There are a number of organisation which aim to help writers of every genre, and many of them also organise prizes and awards. I have described some of the most relevant below.

The Society of Authors will help novice members with contracts, and advise on any legal problems of authorship. It awards several literary prizes of which the most interesting to romantic novelists is the Betty Trask Award.

The Betty Trask Award is given annually for the best first novel by an author under thirty-five years of age, of a 'traditional or romantic nature'. There is a substantial first prize, and other prizes for the short list of six. For further information, write to the Society of Authors, 84 Drayton Gardens, London, SW10 9SD.

The Catherine Cookson Fiction Prize is for previously unpublished novels of at least 70,000 words. Books must be in the 'Cookson tradition'; strong narrative, good characterisation and authentic background, either historical or contemporary. Published or unpublished writers can submit. The prize is £10,000 plus a possible publishing contract. Details from Transworld Publishers Ltd, 61-63 Uxbridge Road, London W5 5SA. Tel: 0181 579 2652.

'I have found writers to be the most warm and generous people I know in giving their time and advice and friendship in the creative world we share.'

The Romantic Novelists' Association was founded by Denise Robins and Vivian Stuart in 1960. Inside the cover of its quarterly *News* magazine there used to be the following statement:

'The aim of this Association is to use all the means in its power, individually and collectively, to raise the prestige of Romantic Authorship.'

As a past Chairman of the RNA, as it is affectionately called, I can vouch for the fact that the Association carries out its promise. Full membership applies to members who have had one or more romantic novels published. Associate membership is open to publishers, agents, booksellers, librarians etc. www.rna-uk.org.

Meetings are held in London at intervals during the year, with prominent speakers such as editors, best-selling romantic novelists, etc, and with time for informal discussion and shop talk afterwards. There is an annual luncheon in London, regional lunches organised by members in their own localities, a winter party, an occasional one-day seminar and annual weekend conference. The quarterly *News* magazine gives details of all events and talks for those members unable to get to the meetings.

There are two annual RNA awards, which are presented at the annual luncheon in April. *The Major Award* is for the best romantic novel published in the current year. This may be contemporary or historical. It is open to members and non-members, subject to RNA rules, and books may be entered by the author or publisher. See the website for more details.

The Netta Muskett Award, more commonly known now as the *New Writers' Award,* will be of more interest to those who are just starting their writing career. This award is for member-authors who have not yet published a romantic novel. They join the RNA on a yearly basis as new writers, regardless of what they may have published in other fields of writing.

Once accepted for membership, they are required to submit a full-length manuscript during September, for criticism, and for entry into the New Writer's Award Scheme. All manuscripts are read, and detailed comments are sent to each author. If a suitable manuscript is forwarded to a publisher and is subsequently published, that author receives the *New Writers' Award* for that year, and automatically becomes a full member. Full membership status applies to all those who are subsequently published, regardless of whether or not they win the award.

The standard required is high, but the criticism is always constructive and helpful and, where an author shows real talent, every encouragement is given. Membership of the RNA is not restricted to women. There are a number of male authors among the membership, although women far outnumber men in writing romantic fiction, as might be expected.

After publication

Writing a novel doesn't end with the moment you first see it in print, exciting though that is. If it's got the elusive something extra between the covers - in the writing and the content - then a novel can be an investment that far exceeds the initial advance and twice-yearly royalties.

You never know when new dividends will be paid out. Your novel may begin as a modest little paperback or as a more glamorous hardback. From then on, it can go into further printings. It could become a bestseller. It might sell to a television company, or a film company might take out an option on the film rights. It's been more than just a dream for some.

Your book could sell to an American publisher, to a book club, to a large print publisher, to countries worldwide. I've had many a pleasant surprise when a new offer comes in for a book I thought was 'dead' and a new edition is printed somewhere in the world. One of them has even been published in Hebrew. There may also be audio sales.

Manga/Comic book

Manga, or comic-book publishing, is a phenomenal success story in Japan, with teenagers dressing up as their favourite characters in shopping malls and subways all over the country. Topics range from vampires to dragons to cartoon characters - and also romance.

I have now published 110 books of all kinds, including many regional novels as Rowena Summers, and wartime sagas as Rachel Moore. Now I am also published in Japanese Manga after a Japanese literary agency contacted me, to say that Ohzora Publishing wanted to adapt three of my early romances, each as a Manga paperback, a magazine one-shot, and an e-book.

The first of these to appear in print is *The Kissing Time* by Jean Saunders. This was originally a Silhouette book published in the USA in 1982 - and has just resurfaced as a Manga book in 2011 - twenty-nine years later.

PLR

Many years after its original publication, your novel could still be earning money for you, thanks to PLR, the long fought for Public Lending Right which allows authors of books borrowed free from public libraries to gain some reward for their pains. On the basis of records kept in a sample selection of libraries across the UK, the PLR office calculates a national borrowing average for each individual title. A loan earns just over one penny and payments are made only on titles earning £1 or more. There is a £6,600 current annual limit per author.

In the few years since PLR came into being, authors of romantic and historical fiction have been delighted to discover that their books are amongst the most borrowed of all - the figures prove it. So, as soon as your novel is published and you are eligible to register for PLR, contact the Public Lending Right Office, Richard House, Sorbonne Close, Stockton-on-Tees TS17 6DA. If you don't register, you won't get any money!

And finally . . .

The mechanics of writing a romantic novel can be summed up neatly enough. Yet, once the mechanics start to show, the illusion of reality is lost. A romance is perhaps no more than that, a convincing illusion which offers a glimpse into the glamorous, the poignant, the racy, the tragic, the passionate. The characters we create are larger than life, for we can meet the people next door every day. Pleasant though they may be, the romantic fiction reader seeks to be transported into a different world from her everyday, familiar one, yet still with that feeling that everything that happens between the pages of the romantic novel could happen to her . . .

Reading is a personal, private experience, and so is the writing of any novel. But it's far more than that once the book is published and becomes public property.

A successful author must be a businesswoman, an accountant, her own publicity person, ahead of her time in seeing the trends of fiction, which change like a capricious breeze. She must be capable of checking contracts, be available for signing sessions, and be ready to speak to women's groups, at luncheons and at seminars if asked. An agent will take care of some of these things, but unless the author chooses to live an ivory tower existence, she will want to be involved in these peripheral activities.

The best help of all in becoming an author lies within ourselves, in that wonderful asset we call our imagination, where we can be transported forward or back in time to suit our stories. Our dreams can let us revive old memories and create new ones. In our heads and our hearts we can be eighteen again at will, with all the delights and pleasures and uncertainties of that particular age.

We share with our heroines their most perfect moments. We fall in love with every one of our heroes, because we will have given him those qualities we most admire. We can rid ourselves of our real life hang-ups, by writing them out through an unsavoury character. We are truly the fortunate ones, to be paid for living out our dreams.

Yet, far more than any other writers, romantic novelists are often quoted out of context in the press, introduced on radio and TV interviews with a few choice phrases meant to titillate the listeners. But still we do it. We write the books that satisfy a million readers. But even more than that, we write the books that satisfy ourselves.

You won't agree with everything I've said in this book, and rightly so. You must decide to write with your own voice. But if some of it has made you think that you too could write romantic fiction, then both of us have reached a happy ending.

And for you, dear reader, I hope it will be as wonderful a beginning as it was for me.

Summing Up

- Join a reputable writers' class. Don't waste time on one that is all praise with no helpful criticism.

- Subscribe to writing magazines. Their advice is invaluable.

- Swanwick and other conferences will inspire you, and in the company of other writers, you will realise you are not alone.

- Be positive. Never give up your dream of becoming an author.

Help List

Journals of Interest to Romantic Novelists

- Writers' News (Editor, Jonathan Telfer)
  5th Floor, 31-32 Park Row, Leeds, LS

- Writing Magazine
  As Writers' News above.

- Writers' Forum (Editor, Carl Styants)
  Select Publisher Services Ltd, PO Box 6337, Bournemouth, BH1 0EH

The Publishers

British Publishers, Romance/Romantic Fiction

Queries on current requirements are advisable before submitting, especially to publishers marked *

- Robert Hale Ltd
  Clerkenwell House, 45-47 Clerkenwell Green, London EC1R 0HT.

- Harlequin Mills & Boon Ltd*
  Eton House, 18-24 Paradise Rd, Richmond, Surrey, TW9 1ZR.

- HarperCollins
  77-85 Fulham Palace Road, London W6 8JB.

- Headline Book Publishing Co
  338 Euston Road, London NW1 3BH.

- Reed International Books, (Mandarin)
  Michelin House, 81 Fulham Road, London, SW3 6RB.

- Hodder & Stoughton
  338 Euston Road, London NW1 3BM.

- Little Brown Book Group (Warner)
  100 Victoria Embankment, London, EC4Y 0DY

- Orion Books
  Orion House, 5 Upper St Martin's Lane, London WC2H 9EA.

- Penguin Books
  5 Windmill St, London W1P 1HF.

- Random House (Century)
  20 Vauxhall Bridge Rd, London SW1V 2SA.

- Severn House Publishers Ltd.
  1st Floor, 9-15 High St, Sutton, Surrey SM1 1DF.

- Simon & Schuster Ltd.
  West Garden Place, Kendal St, London W2 2AQ.

- Transworld Publishers Ltd, (Corgi, Bantam)
  61-62 Uxbridge Rd, London W5 5SA.

- Virgin Publishing Ltd*
  Thames Wharf Studios, Rainville Road, London W6 9HT.

Main US Romance Publisher's Addresses

- Avon Books
  1350 Ave of the Americas, NY10019.

- Ballantine/Fawcett
  201 East 50th St, NY 10022.

- Bantam Books
  1540 Broadway, NY 10036.

- Berkley Publishing Group
  200 Madison Ave, NY 10016.

- Dell
  1500 Broadway, NY 10036.

- Harlequin, NY.
  300 East 42nd St, 6th floor, NY 10017.

- Harlequin, Canada
  225 Duncan Mill Road, Don Mills, Ontario, Canada MOB 3K9.

- Harper Paperbacks
  10 East 53rd St, NY 10022.

- Kensington Books/Zebra/Pinnacle
  850 3rd Ave, NY 10022.

- Leisure Books
  276 5th Ave, NY 10003.

- Pocket Books
  1230 Ave of the Americas, NY 10020.

- Random House/Wings
  40 Engelhard Ave, Avenel NJ 07001.

- St Martin's Press
  175 5th Ave, NY 10003.

- Silhouette
  300 East 42nd St, NY 10017.

- Tor Books
  175 5th Ave, NY 10010.

- Warner Books
  1271 Ave of the Americas, NY 10020.

Main US Romance Organisation

- Romance Writers of America,
  3707 1960 West, Suite 555, Houston, Texas, USA.

Book List

All writers will gradually build up a book list to suit their needs, ranging from the basic dictionary to those that will help to develop their writing expertise. You will amass your own collection and, even if you only use them occasionally, it is good to have them to hand whenever you need them. These are some that I have found most useful or have had recommended to me by others:

- The Writer's Handbook – published annually
- The Writers' and Artists' Yearbook – published annually
- Oxford Writers' Dictionary
- Chambers Dictionary
- Quotations for Our Time – By Dr Laurence Peter
- Fowler's Modern English Usage – OUP
- Chambers Thesaurus
- The Penguin Guide to Punctuation – R L Trask
- Oxford A-Z of Grammar and Punctuation – By John Seeley
- Punctuation – By Graham King
- Good Grammar – By Graham King
- To Writers With Love: Mary Wibberley (Buchan & Enright, 1985).
- The Shell Book of Firsts: Patrick Robertson (Ebury Press, 1983).
- The Penguin Dictionary of Historical Slang: Eric Partridge, abridged by Jacqueline Simpson (Penguin, 1980).
- A Concise History of Costume: James Laver (Thames & Hudson, 1969).
- Costume and Fashion in Colour 1760-1920: Jack Cassin-Scott (Blandford Press, 1971).
- Research for Writers: Ann Hoffman (Midas Books).

- Guinness Book of Names: Leslie Dunkling (Guinness).
- Writing a Novel: John Braine (Eyre & Spottiswoode, 1971).
- Writing Step by Step: Jean Saunders (Allison & Busby).
- Creating Fictional Characters - The Essential Guide: Jean Saunders (Need2Know).
- Writing Dialogue - The Essential Guide: Jean Saunders (Need2Know).
- How to Research Your Novel: Jean Saunders (Allison & Busby).
- Successful Novel Plotting: Jean Saunders (Accent Press).
- Book Proposals - The Essential Guide: Stella Whitelaw (Need2Know).
- The Guide to Book Publishers (Writers' Bookshop, revised annually).

Need - 2 - Know

Available Titles Include ...

Publishing Poetry The Essential Guide
ISBN 978-1-86144-113-3 £9.99

Writing Poetry The Essential Guide
ISBN 978-1-86144-112-6 £9.99

Writing Non-Fiction Books The Essential Guide
ISBN 978-1-86144-114-0 £9.99

Book Proposals The Essential Guide
ISBN 978-1-86144-118-8 £9.99

Writing Dialogue The Essential Guide
ISBN 978-1-86144-119-5 £9.99

Creating Fictional Characters The Essential Guide
ISBN 978-1-86144-120-1 £9.99

Writing Romantic Fiction The Essential Guide
ISBN 978-1-86144-121-8 £9.99

Pilates The Essential Guide
ISBN 978-1-86144-097-6 £9.99

Surfing The Essential Guide
ISBN 978-1-86144-106-5 £9.99

Gardening A Beginner's Guide
ISBN 978-1-86144-100-3 £9.99

Going Green The Essential Guide
ISBN 978-1-86144-089-1 £9.99

Food for Health The Essential Guide
ISBN 978-1-86144-095-2 £9.99

Vegan Cookbook The Essential Guide
ISBN 978-1-86144-123-2 £9.99

Walking A Beginner's Guide
ISBN 978-1-86144-101-0 £9.99

View the full range at **www.need2knowbooks.co.uk**. To order our titles call **01733 898103**,
email **sales@n2kbooks.com** or visit the website. Selected ebooks available online.

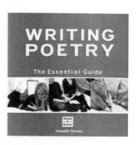

Need - 2 - Know, Remus House, Coltsfoot Drive, Peterborough, PE2 9BF